My Journey:

Seeking God's heart about the truth of homosexuality and what He revealed to me.

By STUART BROWN,
formerly William Stuart Flucas

xulon
PRESS

Copyright © 2015 by Stuart Brown, formerly William Stuart Flucas

My Journey: Seeking God's heart about the truth of homosexuality and what He revealed to me.
by Stuart Brown, formerly William Stuart Flucas

Printed in the United States of America.
Edited by Xulon Press.

ISBN 9781498454032

All rights reserved solely by the author. The author guarantees all contents are original and do not infringe upon the legal rights of any other person or work. No part of this book may be reproduced in any form without the permission of the author. The views expressed in this book are not necessarily those of the publisher.

Unless otherwise indicated, scripture quotations taken from the New King James Version (NKJV). Copyright © 1982 by Thomas Nelson, Inc. Used by permission. All rights reserved.

www.xulonpress.com

Brother David,

May the Lord continue to richly bless and direct you. It was a pleasure meeting you. Be mightily encouraged!

In godly-love,

Stuart Broa

ACKNOWLEDGEMENTS

I wish to thank my Lord and Savior Jesus Christ for His undying love and favor towards me in all ways and in all things. *My Journey* is one way of giving back to Him, making sure He is glorified by its truth which allows Him to work through me in an effort to reach others who are looking to grow deeper in His love on a daily basis. To God be the glory!

FOREWORD

❦

Unless stated otherwise, all scripture references come from the New King James version of the Bible, copyright, 1985, by Thomas Nelson, Inc.

Also, the names of persons used in the book have been changed to protect their privacy.

INTRODUCTION

I am writing this book, a piece born of a longing AND desire to understand homosexual feelings that have always been a part of my psyche for as long as I can remember. I knew it was to God I ultimately would have to take my questions, for I have always known He loves me, and I believe He fashioned me in my mother's womb, just as scripture asserts. So it was to Him I took my question about whether being gay is okay with Him.

My feelings have always been a source of confusion for me, since the young age of five or so, when first I noticed that I was attracted to other boys. I was confused, because it seemed as though everyone besides me liked the opposite sex. So why was I different?

I was born in Southern California, in March of 1968, but my mother, a single, Christian woman raised me in a small farming community in the center of the state. My mother raised my brother and me with occasional help from my grandmother, who lived next door. I am the oldest, and my younger brother, Jeff is one and a half years younger than me. My mother met my dad, Jonson while he was in active duty for the military, and they dated and got pregnant before he deployed for Southeast Asia. Sadly, by the time he returned from active duty, he had become a different person. He decided that he didn't want to be married or raise a son, and years later my mother would discover that his choices were most likely the result of one suffering the effects of post-traumatic stress disorder (PTSD). His decision to leave us left her without a choice about raising a son, so she reluctantly became a single parent. She told me years later that she named me William, because she was fond of Shakespearean plays. But, she only called me William when she was teasing me, haha. She also told me that she made the choice to give me her maternal surname at birth, because she was disappointed in my father's decision to walk away from his responsibility of raising a son. I was called by my middle name growing up, and I liked it better than my first name, so I rarely answered to being called William. She eventually decided to legally change my surname to that of my father's, because she felt later in life I would benefit more by not having her maiden surname. Over time she was able to use her disappointment in my dad's choice to leave us to fuel her own effort to become a great mother. She raised me in a magnanimous, wonderful way. And, this method of raising me in tandem with help from my grandmother and great-grandmother was so effective that I now realize she had successfully found a way to lovingly fill the paternal void in my life that my father had created by leaving us.

A couple of years after I was born my mother met and fell in love with my brother's dad, Jeff Sr., but due to irreconcilable differences that relationship never worked and they divorced after only having been married a short time. My mother worked as a librarian and was able to effectively teach us that faith in God along with reading and writing could help us achieve any dreams that we could imagine. Grandma was always available to babysit during the day, since she worked the night shift as a licensed vocational nurse. If she couldn't babysit us, my great-grandmother, who lived around the corner from us, was always happy to assume the role. All of these wonderful godly women taught me biblical values and mores.

The godly women in my life taught me that God was the maker of the universe, omnipresent, omniscient, and omnipotent. I never questioned that truth. Some people say they don't believe in God, since they have never seen Him, but the question of Him existing was never an issue for me. I once heard an analogy about God that went like this: *How does one know wind exists, for one cannot see wind?* The answer simply enough was: *We can see the effect wind has on the leaves of a tree when it blows through them, so there clearly is an unseen force at work which no one can deny.*

I was also taught that God loves all of His creation, and I remember my childhood minister even declaring back in the late 1970's that mankind was made up of a variety of people, including black, white, handicapped, obese, and, yes, even homosexuals, to name a few. This was a pretty radical statement for a minister to have made in a pulpit back in those days.

I wrote this book in an attempt to ask God directly why He created me as a gay person, if He foreknew the world I was made to live in would ultimately reject me. I am not sure which label a person prefers, but in this book I use the terms *gay* and *homosexual* interchangeably. So I embarked on a journey to ask God directly what He thought about my homosexual inclinations. You will see how He gave me specific answers about homosexuality after I made the decision to truly seek Him as well as read the Bible to completion for the first time in 2004. The answers unfolded over a ten-year period, as I continued to read scripture and listen to what He was showing me.

Some might ask, *Why would anyone read this book and attribute any value to it?* Or better yet, one might posit: *Why would anyone question how he was made in the first place?*

My answer would be that I believe I am a special creation handmade by God Himself. I believe that He first loved me, and He made me to delight myself in His love. There have been many mysterious situations in my life where I wasn't sure what God was saying, but I believe that God will reveal all truth in time. If I am patient enough to journey where He leads me, I know that He will reveal all the answers that concern my heart.

From an early age I heard people say that the Bible condemned homosexuality, so I decided I would avoid reading it. I knew eventually I would have to read the Bible, if I was going to find out what it actually said. I also knew that I would have to pray, so I could get an answer from God that would enable me to live my life in peace. I believe that this journey is one I had to take, since I love God so much, and I realized that I could not have peace in my soul until I knew whether I was living in a way that pleased Him. I had always reacted to the world from the standpoint of living my life based on feelings, a standard that I thought would never mislead me. So, I embarked on this journey, as I needed concrete answers about what God's will was for me.

CHAPTER ONE

If I go back to the beginning of my journey, I believe there were three distinct stages I went through where my mindset changed about how I viewed my sexuality. The first stage, around the age of five or so, was crucial in my developing view of self, for it was here that I first became conscious I was attracted to other boys. I determined that society would have a hard time accepting that I was gay, so I began to tell myself that my feelings would go away if I simply ignored them. During this stage I was so concerned about what other people thought about me, I discovered that hiding my feelings would most likely be the best way to fix the problem.

About a decade and a half later upon turning twenty years old, I realized that I could not change my same gender attraction, so I began to consciously believe that being normal meant accepting my amorous feelings for men. I knew that doing this would allow me to feel like a complete person. I call this stage two in my developing view of self. My happiness at this time became more important than my desire to simply please others. It was also during this stage that I became sexually active. As I continued to mature, I began to realize more and more that I ultimately cared only what God thought about my attraction to men.

Meanwhile, I was attending a church in San Francisco, led by a lesbian pastor, where most of the members were gay. It was here that I decided I would believe that God had definitely made me gay. However, I had consciously chosen to not read the Bible for myself on the issue, because I had a feeling that possibly all of the vitriol I had heard about God's view of gays might be validated in scripture. I was always taught that if you read the Bible, you are responsible for what you read, so I consciously avoided reading it.

I learned to be relatively comfortable in my newfound identity, but after taking a job transfer to the East Coast and leaving my church, my desire to be clear about how God felt about homosexuality reached a climax. I had just turned thirty-six years old, and I realized that I was at a place where I had to get a direct answer from God Himself, so I could finally be at peace about how He made me; this was stage three.

The aforementioned three stages encompass my entire development in reference to my sexuality. Throughout this book, I will refer to God and Jesus interchangeably. I will also use the designation of 'right' to refer to people who believe that homosexuality is morally reprehensible. Conversely, the term 'left' will refer to people who believe that God makes a person gay, therefore being gay is okay with God. This is my journey.

The first conscious memory I have of a 'budding' gay identity was when I was about five years old, standing in line with my mother at a grocery store in San Francisco, the city we lived in at the time. We had moved there a couple of years after I was born. I distinctly remember a handsome guy standing directly behind us at the checkout line. I kept glancing at him, and I recall that my thoughts centered around wishing he was my father. I longed for a male figure to nurture me, just as my mother always did.

Growing up with only a mother made not having a father difficult in many ways. Some people on the right say that this longing for a father is why I became homosexual. They say that my desire to have a father somehow became twisted, which plunged me headlong into developing a homosexual identity. They say that a single female parent raising a boy is a recipe for disaster, since a mother cannot show a male child how to be a man.

Chapter One

I believe that a mother can teach a boy what it means to be a man, but I also believe that a child needs both parents. So, I don't believe the logic to be sound that says a single woman can't raise a man. This is because there are many gay men who were raised in single-parent households, but instead of the father being absent, the mother was absent, and the children also turned out to be gay later in life. I have acquaintances who fit this example.

My mother explained the 'birds and the bees' to me when I was old enough, but my attraction to boys started way before we ever had that talk. I also attended sex education class in grade school, but it was clear that whenever the topic of sex came up, I didn't see or hear anyone validating that it was okay for a boy to love another boy. So, I sensed that I would have to learn about myself another way.

A few years later, I recall several instances where I was approached by men in social settings, like public restrooms and parks, and these men appeared to be looking for sexual favors. Although I didn't totally understand what was happening in these interactions, I knew that the attention men sometimes gave me in public places simply didn't feel right.

The first time I was approached by a man in public happened when my brother and I were riding the bus from San Francisco to a small town in the center of the state where I was raised. While riding, we were seated next to an older man. He seemed to be approximately sixty years old or so, and I was about nine years old at the time. He would purposely rub my left thigh with the outside of his right hand, as I sat in the middle seat between him and my brother. He would make eye contact with me and smile; nothing else happened, but I never forgot that moment.

Sadly, I think the public at large thinks that homosexuality is synonymous with pedophilia, but I am not sure if these men are gay at all. What I know about pedophilia is that the perpetrator feels they lack control in life, thus they must control what is perceived as a weaker target to feel powerful. It is not about sex.

Conversely, I believe that homosexuality is about being attracted to a life partner who happens to be of the same gender.

The second time I was approached by a man was when my mother, brother and I were having lunch at a seafood restaurant at the wharf in San Francisco. I was about ten years old or so at the time. Just to the right of me, I noticed an appreciably older man, probably about fifty years old, sitting at a table adjacent to ours. He kept looking at me and smiling, so I smiled back. Moments later, I had to use the bathroom, so my mother allowed my brother and me to leave and find the nearest men's bathroom. During our walk, I had the feeling that something wasn't right. As we walked to the bathroom, I felt as though I was being watched. When I turned around, I noticed that the older man from the nearby table appeared to be following us, still smiling; I immediately felt terror.

I remember that after we entered the bathroom, the man stood near the entrance to the bathroom, simply smiled, and appeared to be waiting. I instructed my brother to hurry up, so we could get back to where Mom was. That experience would be the first of about five episodes I recall from childhood, where I had been approached sexually by a boy or man. When we returned to the table with my mother, I told her about it, and she was very concerned.

The third instance occurred while I was playing on a jungle gym in a local park in my hometown. I guess I was about eleven years old at the time. My grandmother was chaperoning us, and I had to use the bathroom. As I walked to the bathroom, a boy of about sixteen years of age walked over to me as I tried to enter the bathroom, and asked me if I wanted to 'play'. I somehow knew that play inferred something involving sex or some sort of play that was unacceptable, because of his facial expression and the tone of his voice.

As a little boy, I do remember playing 'doctor' and 'truth or dare' with my cousins, for I think it was an attempt to make sense of the discussions we all had with our parents as well as

Chapter One

with school teachers about human sexuality. But while playing these games, we never disrobed or engaged in sexual behavior. We just talked and told jokes.

The boy at the playground bathroom who wanted to play wanted something else, though, because the look in his eye made me feel that he wanted to do something that was illegal or immoral. So, I declined and ran back to my grandmother and told her about the incident. She was gravely concerned. She went to look for the boy, but he had vanished.

The fourth instance happened just after our family moved out of my grandmother's home into our newly built family home next door. During one particular instance, a cousin related by marriage named Ryan came to visit us with his wife Angela, his best friend David, and David's girlfriend Donna. In those days we always left our back door unlocked when we were home, so grandma wouldn't have to knock when she came over and vice versa. While Ryan, Angela, Donna and my mother were next door at my grandmother's house, David returned to our house and entered. He then knocked on my bedroom door which I customarily kept closed for privacy, and he entered after I had said that it was okay for him to do so. He asked me questions about my life, and I remember showing him my model dinosaurs and telling him about my trophies from baseball. He then told me how attractive I was, grabbed me by the waist and French kissed me.

It was the first time I had ever kissed anyone romantically in the mouth, let alone a man. Although it felt good, confusion erupted, as new emotions flooded my brain. I told him I had to leave, and I ran out of the house and sought consolation in the presence of my pet pig, which was in my aunt's backyard, one house over from ours. I was about fourteen years old at the time. I immediately told my mother about the situation when she returned from my grandmother's house next door, and she was furious. She said she needed to confront Ryan and David, so she gathered Angela, Donna, and myself, so the six of us could sit and discuss what had occurred.

Ryan was about thirty-five years old, Angela was about thirty-three, David was about thirty-four, and Donna was also about thirty-four at the time. I remember collapsing in tears, as Ryan, Angela, David and Donna all flatly rejected my version of events, even though the only people present during the incident were David and myself.

David's friends told my mother that I was a liar, and I couldn't believe that David had the temerity to stare me down with a look on his face that made me feel he might be saying, "good luck proving that what you are saying is true." My mother never allowed David to visit our house again.

On a different occasion, next door at my grandmother's house, I observed that same cousin, Ryan, continually looking at the crotch of my pants and those of my male cousins' whenever he would talk with us. At the time I didn't understand the behavior, so I expressed to my mother that I was uncomfortable in Ryan's company, also. My mother then decided that Ryan would never be allowed to visit our house again either. People outside of me apparently saw something in me that others didn't, but this gave them no right to take advantage of my innocence. To this day I don't believe that the abuse I suffered at the hands of these men had anything to do with why I am gay. I believe it had to do with the fact that they saw something in me and simply abused me, because I was innocent. I now know how vulnerable young people are. Adults are charged with taking care of them, not abusing them.

Again, I assert that these events had nothing to do with why I was attracted to men. I think it is possible that abuse contributes to a person's development, but I believe the sexual identity that we grow into is determined even before birth. I will talk more about that later.

CHAPTER TWO

After the events of my youth, I refined a coping mechanism of dealing with my budding homosexuality by ignoring my feelings and not dealing with them. I didn't have the courage to accept my attraction to men, for I felt that society would not understand. I continued hiding my attraction, and I eventually began lying about it to myself and others. This continued until I reached dating age, as I made every effort to learn to like girls.

Throughout my development, I sensed that my mother knew I was struggling with something, but I wasn't ready to tell her. Relatives would say I was becoming very attractive and they wondered why I didn't have a girlfriend. However, Mom would always tell them that I was more interested in school than girls at the time, for my interest in romance would come later.

Around this time, I remember exchanging pictures at school on picture day with friends, and I kept a picture in the top drawer of my clothes chest of a friend named Seamus, a guy whom I had developed a serious crush on during eighth grade. I used to give the picture a kiss every night before bed, and I always hoped my brother never saw me doing it, because his bunk bed was directly behind me when I stood at the chest of drawers. At school, I used to wrestle playfully with Seamus in the hallways, and we both lit up with smiles every time we encountered each other. Seamus was dating girls, but I knew I was falling in love with him.

My Journey: Seeking God's heart about the truth of homosexuality and what He revealed to me.

I was turning fourteen years old, and I was upset about being attracted to him, because I somehow knew the feelings weren't mutual. I also felt like I was the only person in the world who felt this way. I definitely knew I could not talk to Seamus about how I was feeling. However, I also couldn't make the feelings go away. I sensed that expressing them would alienate my friends, so I ignored my emotional angst, hoping it would go away on its own. I remember weeping bitterly one night as I looked at the picture of Seamus, and as I lay down to sleep that night, I prayed and asked God to take my life. I felt I simply could not live anymore with the emotional pain of being gay in a world that I perceived would not accept me.

I now know God's answer to my prayer was ABSOLUTELY NOT!, for He has a plan for my life, although I didn't understand that at the time. The fact that I awoke the next morning, despite my prayer, was a clear answer God was not going to let me die. I felt as though God was saying to me that I simply had to learn to deal with my feelings, because reconciling feelings was part of my journey. So, I continued to keep my feelings secret and deny them in an effort to be accepted by people.

Strangely, although I was raised in a Christian household and went to church every Sunday, I was not even aware that the Bible said anything about sexuality, let alone homosexuality. I didn't personally read the Bible as a child, though I was required to memorize excerpts for Sunday school from time to time. I did, however, realize that people outside of church talked about same sex attraction, and they always did so in a disapproving way. So, I decided that I would keep my feelings secret in an effort to preempt people from rejecting me.

I tried in earnest to be above reproach in every other aspect of my being, and I believed this strategy to be the correct one which would enable me to avoid ever having to confront the issue of sexuality in the company of others. I made a concerted effort to be the best at everything in school. I learned to play the alto saxophone in elementary school, and I continued to play it for a few years. My grandmother wanted all of her grandchildren to have a skill that would enrich them all of their lives, so we each learned a musical instrument. In elementary school I became a scout, as I was continually promoted over the years while reaching for the coveted top rank which I ultimately abandoned in pursuit of other goals. A few years later in junior high school, my classmates voted me "most likely to succeed," and I also attained straight A's, graduating with a 4.0 grade point average in conjunction with earning the top school award for scholastic excellence.

During my freshman year of high school, my track and field coach invited me to compete as a junior varsity sprinter and long jumper, since I seemed to have natural ability. I had run track and field since my days in elementary school, and I especially loved the long jump. That year coach invited me to assist him working on the infield of one of the state's largest track and field competitions in the world which was held locally. It allowed me to meet and talk with my favorite track inspirations in person that day. They each let me take pictures with them and ask questions about their respective track and field experiences. I molded myself to be well spoken, polished and fit, just like them; this action would enable me to remain above reproach by those around me. Years later I would see the life story of a famous football player and realize that just as he channeled the pain of being rejected for being an obese child into fuel that made him a star athlete, I was able to use that same strategy in my formative years. However, my fuel was the shame of knowing I was gay. Coping is an interesting thing.

In high school I decided to learn to play the Scottish Highland Bagpipes after my school's brass band, The Regal Red Brigade was asked to play in a welcome concert in honor of the Queen's visit to the Bay Area during that year. She was touring the United States, and several local bagpipe bands as well as my high school brass band were invited to represent the United States by playing for her. My city's local bagpipe band, The Saint Peter's Society Pipe Band was one of the guest performers and listening to them warm up was my first time ever hearing bagpipes in person. I fell in love instantly and vowed to find a way to learn the pipes, myself. After speaking with the Pipe Major, George Pollard, he agreed to teach me piping after we returned to my home town. I immediately walked away from my alto saxophone and worked at becoming a good piper. George taught me lessons at his house weekly, and within a year I joined the band; this was during my freshman year of high school. George lived with his son, Mike, a nice, biracial guy who was about my age. George told me in time that he had met Mike's mother, a black American woman while he was visiting the United States from Scotland. He fell in love with her, married, and they had Mike; they later divorced. Mike never wanted to learn the pipes, so my decision to study the pipes brought George unspeakable joy, because his heart's desire was for his son to learn the obscure skill of piping.

My grandmother urged me to take private jazz alto saxophone lessons from a friend of hers who was also a local celebrity and radio announcer, a man named Mack Windham. Mack often toured Europe with his small band while performing, but when he was home in the United States I went to his house a few times for lessons. But, my heart just wasn't in it.

My high school hosted a couple of exchange students from Europe on a popular exchange student program while I was in high school; their names were Anna and Maia. Since I was already feeling a bit of an outcast with regard to my romantic feelings toward boys, I found it natural to befriend the foreign girls, as I made a concerted effort to be comfortable around other people who were perceived to be different. Anna and Maia returned to Europe after their year was over, but their visit had inspired me to also dream of becoming a foreign exchange student. I also applied to become an exchange student, and I was sent to Australia under an American student exchange program in 1985 during my junior year of high school. I was the only American to have ever gone abroad in my school's history which was a huge milestone for me. My high school lacked an exchange program, but I befriended other applicants from a nearby city whose management sheltered me under

Chapter Two

their local chapter. I was also able to disprove my guidance counselor, Helena's affirmation that I would never be able to accomplish the goal of going abroad. Her attempt to discourage me from becoming an exchange student fueled me even more to become successful in this endeavor. I had to prove her wrong, and I thank God that I was allowed to do so, which also proved to me that I could do anything I could imagine.

One day while piping in the exchange student contingent of the national parade, I guess a cameraman noticed me, because the next morning Mum ran into my room and woke me up, showing me how I had made front page news while piping and wearing my kilt from the previous day. I tried to remain above reproach by being the best at everything I could muster, so people wouldn't see who I really was. It was an amazing journey living 'Down Under', but in spite of all my trying, I still couldn't outrun my feelings there either. However, through piping, I had achieved another lifetime goal of doing something that I really enjoyed.

The host family that welcomed me included two parents and three children. The parents, Adam and Gwen gave me the option of calling them by their first names or calling them Mum and Dad, so I chose the latter. I was the eldest of the children at sixteen years old, along with my sister Carmine who is one month younger than I am. Our younger brother Alvin was fourteen years old, and our youngest sister, Adaline was twelve years old at that time. Dad taught me how to tie a necktie, and his having taught me that skill proved to be an indelible experience I will never forget. Mum was a master homemaker, and she and Dad prepared me well for life in Australia. Even though they prepared me well, the impenetrable wall I had erected around my emotions was fracturing and beginning to crumble. I figured if I could get people to like me for my myriad accomplishments, they would choose to ignore my dirty little secret. As my dirty little secret metastasized inside, I developed a crush on my big sister's boyfriend, Dilbert, while I was living there. Dilbert and I became best friends, and I spent the night at his house at times. I was so infatuated with him that I often found myself watching him sleep, as I lay in a twin bed which was adjacent to his twin bed. I also had a few other crushes while attending the private Catholic all boys' school I attended, but as usual I continued to deny my feelings by telling myself that my feelings would go away over time. Little did I know that denying my amorous feelings would prove to be disastrous for me down the road.

CHAPTER THREE

I call the next juncture of my life stage two, for this is where I realized that the barrier I had erected to hide my homosexual feelings from myself and others was not working, as the wall began to topple and fall. One year after returning from Australia, I graduated high school and began college at a local California State University campus. I had just turned eighteen years old; I had moved back in with my mom and was living at home. A couple of years after having moved home, I was doing well in school, but I was dying emotionally as the fractured coping mechanisms that lay deep inside continued to operate erratically. My feelings simply began to bleed through, and I no longer had the strength to hold them back, as I noticed my facial expressions began to betray the effort of holding them. It was especially difficult to be around guys to whom I was sexually attracted. In an effort to salvage a bit of normalcy around my emotions, I rejoined the pipe band, since piping soothed my emotions. I stayed with the band for about three years longer, as we piped for weddings, funerals, and piping competitions in our 'grade four' category at several Scottish Highland Festivals throughout California. I was attending my freshman year of college at the university campus back then, and I was still a virgin. The only person I had ever kissed was David, and I knew that I wanted to meet a guy, but I simply didn't know how to go about doing it. I felt myself unraveling emotionally, so in an effort to salvage my sanity I made the decision to stop denying my feelings, because no matter how I tried, it wasn't working, anyway. I was only deceiving myself.

During my sophomore year of college, I was working for a shoe company called the Runner's Foot. I found myself feeling like a kid in a candy store, because the guys I worked with, as well as many of the store's patrons, were athletic, handsome, masculine men. I couldn't hide my feelings anymore, and I knew that I would eventually be put in a compromising position wherein my facade would crack and the truth about me would be known. A colleague at the time, Dean, flirted with me at work. He was the first guy in my age bracket that I was attracted to who realized I was gay.

We were allowed to play only sports-themed videos in the store, but since the manager was out of the store that day, we rebelled and played a popular war film. There was a shower scene where the star of the film removed his shirt, so I made a comment to Dean, who was the only other person in the store with me at the time, that I didn't understand what the big deal was about the star's sex appeal.

Dean obviously sensed my interest in men and his response was, "Well, I would suck his dick any day." I was shocked. The cat was definitely out of the bag now! This was the first real conversation I had had with another man about my same gender attraction. I had joked with guys in Australia about male sex, but they were always jokes. This time was real, and I was on unfamiliar ground.

I knew Dean was laying a trap for me, but I hadn't anticipated how the rest of our interaction might play out. I clearly wanted Dean to be attracted to me, but I didn't know how to deal with the situation. Later in the day, Dean wrestled with me in the stock room and picked me up, cradling me in his arms. He wouldn't let me down for a minute or so, as he just gazed at me like a cat toying with a mouse. He just grinned at me playfully knowing that because he was stronger, I could only get out of his grasp, if he allowed it. An hour or so later, he repeatedly squeezed past me and purposely grazed my posterior with his crotch as he passed. I

Chapter Three

could feel his breath on my neck, and I again noticed that familiar look in his eye that reminded me of the men who had taken notice of me when I was younger.

I was studying martial arts at the time and had recently earned my brown belt in Korean karate. But, I had always wanted to study and learn the samurai sword after I'd seen a famous Japanese samurai epic that Hollywood adapted and made into a popular western. I saw the film a few years earlier while watching samurai films which came on television every Saturday. While looking in the newspaper, I found a Japanese sword collector in the want ads and was able to buy my first machine-made blade from him as well as learn the basic lessons of the sword art, kenjutsu. He was not a certified teacher, so I decided to wait until I could find a teacher who was a master of the skills I wanted to acquire. I realized a seed was planted regarding the sword when I saw the samurai movie, and I knew I couldn't rest until I would be able to learn the samurai arts. I started taking karate classes right after returning from Australia, for I felt that every man needs to know how to throw a punch. Even though my mother studied judo briefly in junior college, I knew she couldn't teach me to throw a punch.

Dean wanted to learn a few techniques that might aid him with his wrestling skill at college, so to be alone we decided to drive to my house, since my mother was still at work. I showed him a few karate moves in the backyard, and he reciprocated by showing me a few wrestling moves. When he pinned me on my back and looked deep into my eyes like he had in the store, the sexual tension began to mount. My discomfort forced me to break out of his embrace, and I suggested we go back in the house. I gave Dean a beer, and he relaxed and reclined on my bed. Although I was still a virgin and sexually ignorant, I could sense he was asking me to have sex with him, as he constantly held my gaze.

I was frozen and simply didn't know what to do. In my discomfort, I let the moment pass, as I focused on simply engaging him further in conversation. He finally excused himself and decided to go home, I am sure, because he realized that nothing sexual was going to happen. As he left, I tried to kiss him goodbye, but he panicked, pushed me away and asked me what I was doing. My confusion only escalated, because I thought he was interested in me. Why did he reject me now, after having seduced me only moments ago? I simply wondered what was the hurry and why couldn't our interaction simply unfold slower?

The next day at work, Dean acted as if the whole incident was a figment of my imagination, and he treated me coldly. His girlfriend dropped by the store, and he made a point of kissing her in front of me while looking at me out of the corner of his eye. His look made me feel like he was saying, "I am really straight." Later in the day, I confronted him, asking him what was wrong, but his reply was that he was in love with his girlfriend and that he wasn't gay. It was abundantly clear that I was alone in how I was feeling. I pondered the question: If there were others in the world like me, how did they develop healthy, loving relationships?

A few months later, I remember being approached by a bisexual woman in my humanities study group at school, who quizzed me about my sexuality. She said that she knew I was gay, confessed to me that she was lesbian, and she asked if I wanted to go to a gay bar as a social outing. She was married to a bisexual man and they had two children, though I found her admission a bit odd. The husband insisted on meeting me first, to make sure I had no romantic interest in his wife, so I met them at their house, and had a brief conversation about going out to the bar. Even though venturing out and exploring this part of myself felt weird, I knew that being at her house would enable me to learn more about myself. So I sought this woman for answers as to what was happening to me.

I recall that it was a Friday night she wanted to meet me at the bar. However, as I got ready to go later that night, she called and said she couldn't go out, because her husband was jealous of her going to the bar with me and wanted her to stay home. Since my interest was really piqued by all of my experiences up until this

Chapter Three

point, I decided that even though I was scared, I was determined not to let this moment pass. This woman had in one conversation successfully broken down the remainder of my defenses, so I felt that going to the gay bar would be the only remedy which would allow me to feel like I was complete.

The bar was called the Courageous Steer. It was near my home town, and I heard people make jokes about it in passing. As I sat in the parking lot, summoning the courage to enter, I began to sweat. I was paralyzed with fear at the thought of what I might find inside the bar. People on the right always said that gays were perverted, so my imagination ran wild at what I might find inside the bar, but I finally found the courage and went in. Shortly after getting through the door, I stood in the hallway, since I was afraid to enter the main room. A minute or two later, a man who looked to be in his sixties approached me, clad in a black leather cap, black leather jacket, white t-shirt, black leather pants, and black leather boots. He had a strong European accent, and I was terrified, as I thought, "What could this old man want from me?"

His appearance betrayed his demeanor, because he said simply that he was the owner, and asked me if I was old enough to be in the bar legally. I said yes and showed him my driver's license. He said that he had not seen me there before, so he invited me to relax, come in and have a good time. His casual approach alleviated my nervousness. Although I didn't know what to expect upon entering the main room, I was surprised to find a fellow classmate, Sandra from my history class, standing across the dance floor from me. In my astonishment, I ran over to her, and marveled at how we had run into each other at such an unexpected place. I sensed Sandra was a lesbian, but it simply wasn't a question you would ask someone in those days.

Sandra became a closer friend over time, who would meet my mother and stay overnight from time to time. She would drive to my house, and we would go to the bars together, even driving as far as the Bay Area on the weekend nights while each taking turns driving our respective cars. We shared our experiences of knowing how we felt growing up, and we went to the bars most weekends to dance, as we sought release from the self-imposed walls that we each had cast upon ourselves. Sandra found a girlfriend, so we began to spend less time together and eventually fell out of touch. But, it was this experience of being in the presence of another loving, wonderful soul who happened to be gay that I concluded my attraction to men was normal. This helped me finally integrate my gay feelings into my psyche.

During this time, I finally decided that my mother needed to understand why there was emotional distance between us. I had pushed her away at times, because I was not ready to reveal my secret. So, I decided it was time to inform her of my lifelong struggle. I sat her down at the dinner table in the kitchen one night and told her that I had something sensitive to share, which she might not like. It was liberating to finally let her in on my secret. She pondered the revelation, then after a moment of thinking, said, "Well, believe it or not, I used to dress you in pretty colors, so I wonder if that had anything to do with it?" She also said that she used to allow a transvestite friend of hers to babysit us while she was at work at times while we lived in San Francisco; she wondered if that might be the reason I felt this way. She went on to say, "But you're my son, I love you, and you don't steal or kill, so how does this affect our relationship?"

She also remarked how, as a mother, she was concerned for my welfare, since I would be living in a world that would most likely hate me. I made it clear to her that I was not concerned about my own safety; I was only concerned how this revelation might scar or sully the family name. It was so nice to finally have the support of the person I loved most in the world. However, I realized over time that her approval alone would not be enough to help me navigate the deep, dangerous waters of living a life opposite the mainstream in late 1980's America.

CHAPTER FOUR

Years later, after having 'come out of the closet', dating men and occasionally having sex without love, I began to lose control of myself and became increasingly sexually immoral. I often heard people on the right talk about how immoral gay people were, but I never understood why gay people were any more immoral than straight people.

I believed a lot of the vitriol stemmed from their fear of the unknown. However, that doesn't mean that any human being has the right to stand in judgement of another. I think historically gay people have become scapegoats for people looking to cover up their own sin. It is interesting to note the human tendency to blame others for something, though you yourself might be guilty of doing or wanting the same thing. I think of the Nazis in Germany, and how they made the Jews the scapegoats for the lack of jobs, for example. So, the Nazis systematically targeted and killed Jews which assuaged their fears. They also targeted and labeled gays by putting a pink triangle on their homes, so they could be identified easily by the Third Reich. I always wondered why an evil group like the Nazis would seek out and kill another group that was purportedly evil. I reasoned that since the Nazis were evil then being gay must be godly. For why would an evil group search out and kill another group that was also evil? It just didn't seem logical to me.

My logic at the time then led me to the conclusion that gay people must therefore be normal and had the blessing of God on their lives. I remember having heard that the Bible says we are all sinners, while I was growing up in the church. But why is this supposed sin of homosexuality so bad? Or is it only bad in the context of how it is practiced? These were the questions I began to ask myself. However, up until this time, I still had not read the Bible for myself. And I had not consciously asked God, because I was deducing that I was made to be gay. People on the right say that God has a problem with homosexuality, so I pondered: Would gay marriage take care of the issue of morality for God, if people on the right were in fact correct about God hating homosexuality?

I didn't believe that I was any more immoral than anyone else, but it had become clear to me that I was losing control of my sexual appetite and behavior, and I needed to learn how to regulate myself. Soon after coming out, I fell off a steep precipice with regard to sexual behavior. Quite simply, I needed to make sure I had a good parachute or I would crash land. Simultaneously, I realized that I hadn't spoken further to God about my sexuality since the night I had asked Him to end my life, when I was fourteen years old. Somehow, I still felt that God was covering and protecting me from all harm and danger, in spite of my choices.

I left my home town in 1989 at the end of my sophomore year and transferred to San Francisco where I attended another university campus, since it had an international relations program that my previous university lacked. I transferred my Runner's Foot salesman job to San Francisco and worked just down the street from my dormitory.

One day at work, a handsome man entered the store after having walked by a few times to 'cruise' me (undress me with his eyes), a gay term. He eventually entered the store and browsed the shoe section while flirting with me. So, I approached and asked how I could help him. So, he teased me a bit saying that he wanted to try on different pairs of shoes, but I knew he had

Chapter Four

more on his mind than shoes. He ended up trying on a pair of shorts that were too small for him. He was tall, blond, and had an amazing physique. He then asked me, clearly flirting, if I would give him my opinion of the shorts when he exited the dressing room. It turns out he was a dancer in a famous ballet company, and when he exited the room I nearly fainted. I had never seen such a beautiful man in my life; his legs were amazingly muscular and defined. He bought the shorts, and when I had given him the change from buying the shorts, he held my gaze and grasped my fingers as I put the change in his hand.

The store manager and assistant manager, both gay, told me to ask for his phone number, but all I could think about was how my experience with Dean a year or so earlier did not go very well. Plus, I was at work and he was the customer. Also, I somehow knew he wanted sex but probably was not interested in a relationship. The desire to build a monogamous relationship is really what has always fueled me. This was also the year when the Human Immunodeficiency Virus (HIV) became widely known. Before I knew it, I was grieving every few months for acquaintances who had succumbed to Acquired Immunodeficiency Syndrome (AIDS).

On weekends I was going to all of the gay nightclubs and bars, only to leave frustrated, because I was not connecting emotionally with other gay men. I believe the late 1980's were about letting go of sexual repression, and no one appeared to be interested in developing monogamous unions. Since I couldn't connect with another man in a monogamous way, I finally decided that I might as well proceed with having sex with strangers every now and again, until I was able to find a partner to love. Rumors about the Bible's prohibition of homosexuality continually scared me, but I persisted in choosing not to read it.

After graduation in January 1991, I moved off campus, and I filed Chapter 7 bankruptcy after having gotten into a little credit card debt. I then moved into a two-bedroom apartment with an old boyfriend who had become one of my closest platonic friends.

He would often leave the house and go for a drive before bedtime, and I always heard him leave the house and wondered where he ventured. Our rooms were adjacent, so I would often hear him come in late after the drive. He later told me that he frequented bookstores and bathhouses and had casual sex with men, which allowed him to sleep better; having casual sex for him was the equivalent of taking a sleeping pill. As I became more curious about where he went every other night, I finally asked if I could tag along; it was a huge mistake.

I began to see how sin had established deep roots in my life, though I thought I could handle any fallout which might result from any erroneous choices. My grandmother used to have a carved wooden statue of three monkeys which sat on her dining room shelf next to her thimble collection. It symbolized how people are supposed to guard their eyes, ears and mouth. She always used to say "see no evil, hear no evil and speak no evil". This is a biblical principle, but I was still too immature to understand that I was setting myself up for failure by wanting to tag along with Greg on his nightly outings. I eventually got to the point where I would look forward to going to the bookstores, and I eventually started to go without him. I continued this behavior for many years, even after our roommate situation ended.

Sin is a terrible thing. It creeps in like a best friend, takes up residence and hardens our hearts to the truth. More and more I began to realize that I needed to have a litmus test for determining what was acceptable behavior, if I was going to live my life as a gay man. By thinking I was in control, before I knew it, I had become addicted to sex; I simply didn't know how to stop. I began having sex with multiple men on a daily basis, and even though it was mostly oral in nature, I knew the behavior was wrong. Also the fact that one might be able to contract hiv didn't seem to hinder me. Eventually I began to notice that whenever I would arrive at an adult bookstore to have sex with strangers, an ambulance was leaving. If I was leaving the bookstore afterwards, an ambulance would be arriving. I never really figured it

Chapter Four

out until years later, but I now believe it was God showing me even then that those places were not where He wanted me to be. I believe the ambulance symbolized danger, and it was a solemn reminder that if I didn't stop what I was doing, I would also be hauled away in one of those ambulances.

How beautiful it was that I was spared from whatever horrible things were happening in those places and others. I had heard stories of people being raped, stabbed and even killed in the stores I went to, so it was amazing to learn I was being kept safe. I don't believe that being protected was an accident, either, for I knew God had a plan for my life. People who know me well say that I always attribute spiritual significance to my life experiences, and I agree that they could be right. I don't believe there are accidents in life. I believe I am a spirit who possesses a soul and who lives in a body. I believe that God loved me and planned my life out before the earth was even formed, and He lovingly placed me inside my mother's womb at conception.

1991 was also the year that I would begin formal kenjutsu lessons, as I felt I needed to add to my karate skills which would help me control my emotions better and also prepare me, should I ever need to defend myself in a fight. During a brief stint working part time at a movie theater, a colleague gave me a flyer he found on a telephone pole that advertised kenjutsu lessons. I couldn't believe I had actually run into an opportunity to potentially learn the sword! Through my theater colleague, I had finally found a teacher who taught the samurai sword; I felt like this was a sign from God that I was meant to study and master kenjutsu. The sensei, which means teacher in Japanese, had formulated his own special system of kenjutsu born of three disparate ancient ryu which means school in Japanese. He combined the ancient mainland samurai battle style with a more regional style; he added sparse ninjutsu tactics which rounded out the system. So, I hoped the teacher would accept and teach me; I even told him I was gay, because I wanted to make sure I was welcome in his home and in his classes. Learning the sword was the biggest goal in life at that time, and my sword teacher was a master of the art who was originally from Japan. The sword became a big part of my identity, and God would eventually show me that attaching such importance to anything outside of Him only pushed me further and further away from Him.

CHAPTER FIVE

My first permanent full-time job after graduation was that of associate operations specialist for a prominent stock brokerage firm in downtown San Francisco. By this time, I noticed that I had developed anxiety, which I somehow knew was rooted in the fact that I had ignored my deepest feelings around sexuality. I also believe my wanton sexual behavior was contributing to my anxiety, but I didn't know how to fix it. I thought that becoming sexually active would alleviate any discomfort I had around being gay. However, the bedroom was only part of my problem. My refusal to completely accept my sexuality, in spite of the fact I was being sexually active, allowed the anxiety to flourish. I noticed in social situations that I had unresolved tension that I couldn't pinpoint or alleviate.

One morning, upon entering a staff meeting around eight a.m., I had a panic attack, began to sweat profusely, and couldn't breathe. My colleagues knew that I was asthmatic, so they got my asthma inhaler out of my desk, thinking it was what I needed. Using the inhaler only made the attack worse, so the boss called the paramedics. When the paramedics arrived, they asked if I had taken any medication. Upon finding that I had used my inhaler, they informed me that taking the inhaler only made the attack worse, since it was adrenaline. I didn't know what was happening to me, so I asked the paramedic if I was having heart failure. He explained matter-of-factly that I was having a panic attack and that medicine was not the cure. He suggested I contact my employee assistance program through human resources and speak with a counselor, because panic attacks are derived from some emotional problem that is rearing itself.

I now understand that the mind is no different than the rest of the body, and if we go to a doctor to heal the body, then we need to go to a doctor to heal the mind. I was born into the African American culture, and I viewed therapy as something only other cultures did. My mother believed in therapy, but the culture in general seemed to be steeped in a false sense of pride which said our problems resolved themselves over time, if we simply ignored them. However, deep down inside I knew that entertaining the notion that problems fixing themselves was hopeful at best and dysfunctional at worst. Since God's design of the human body is so amazing, I have learned over time that often all the mind needs are space and time to correct itself, for God is the only real healer. Everyone else is just practicing medicine.

I believe that aligning myself with God is really the best medicine for success. I believe He gives me knowledge and wisdom that enables me to avoid pitfalls from the beginning. At the time, though, I felt that the path to truly integrating my sexuality into my life required psychological counseling. I began seeing a counselor, who prescribed twenty milligrams of antidepressant in conjunction with psychotherapy, which I did for about six months. After the therapy ended, I realized that the anxiety was still present, so I continued to take a dosage of about ten milligrams daily for what turned out to be fifteen or more years. The medicine worked well allowing me to function much as I had before, but I could feel that the anxiety had not really left me.

Medicine along with therapy helped me to examine the issues that led to my emotional discomfort in the first place. The therapist made it clear, however, that medicine was only meant to lessen the anxiety, so I could begin the work of identifying what was really wrong and develop the courage to fix it. I knew

Chapter Five

antidepressants were a short-term fix, and I knew I did not want to be on them forever.

At one point, the anxiety took a downturn and became agoraphobia, and I became uncomfortable around strangers. At first I was uncomfortable around men only, but eventually women unnerved me. I knew that I was getting worse, so I asked my general practitioner to put me into a mental hospital overnight. He agreed, and I went, but it became abundantly clear to me while overnight in the hospital that my problems were not severe enough for me to be there. I remember my roommate that night was so medicated that I don't even believe he knew I was in the room. I didn't sleep much at all that night. Being there was a 'wake up' call that made me realize I simply needed to learn to face the truth of who I was, so I could move on. So, I checked myself out the next day.

My therapist agreed completely, and advised me that the solution to my anxiety was to disclose my sexuality openly at work whenever the situation allowed for it, which would alleviate my anxiety. He said that doing so would allow me to live a fulfilled life. So, in small doses, I did just that. After all, I lived in San Francisco, and if it was okay to be gay anywhere, then it was okay in San Francisco, arguably the gayest city on the planet. So after finally deciding to become sexually active and admit that I was gay in public, I felt that my identity as a gay man was firmly established.

Around this time, it was as if God Himself said, "That's enough," and I remember that my agoraphobia, sexual addiction and need for medication completely left me. I now know what it feels like to be delivered from something. The desire simply vanished. God is amazing. I can't recall if I had specifically asked God to deliver me, but it was clearly what He wanted me to experience. Yet the homosexual feelings didn't go away. So, I felt God was telling me that it was okay to be gay.

Ultimately, I believe that God is the only one who can fix me, for He made me. I can't say that my sexual behavior up until the point of being delivered from promiscuity was infrequent, for I was still being quite promiscuous when he delivered me. So, in looking back, I have to ask: Why did God decide to intervene and deliver me at that time? I am not completely sure, but I do believe His timing is perfect. It's possible that if He did nothing, I would have contracted HIV and wouldn't be here to tell my story.

Foremost, I believe I am a spirit having a fleshly experience not a fleshy being having a spiritual experience. I discovered that aligning myself with God only made more and more sense to me as time progressed. However, I was still lacking in spiritual understanding, and I was not yet at a place where I was willing to examine God's view of my desires, which I sensed would be in the Bible. Yet I was learning to sense Him more and more every day, so it was simply a matter of time before I would want to talk to Him directly again about this issue of sexuality. Since I was raised in a Christian household and wanted God in my life, I decided that I needed to begin the work of finding out what He actually said about homosexuality.

I believed seeking God was the answer to addressing the issue of my lack of comfort regarding my sexuality. This book is about my desire to understand how God made me, but it is also about how I wanted to be obedient to His commands, because deep down in my soul obedience to His will was what I truly desired. I was becoming less and less concerned about what people thought as time went on and became more and more concerned about what my Father in heaven thought. I have no regrets about those earlier years, because even then I believed that God was preparing me for something greater. My experiences made me more resilient, and I was coming to a new realization about how to live, for I became ever more concerned about what God expects from me.

Towards the end of 1998, I was working for another prominent stock market firm in San Francisco, as a mutual funds networking specialist. One day upon heading to work, I stood on the street corner across from my office building, waiting for the light to change, and I noticed a car careening pretty fast down

Chapter Five

the street in a northbound direction. As he sped down the street, a taxi cab coming southbound turned left in front of him and forced him off of the road, and he ran directly into me! I saw the car coming towards me, but I never imagined it would come on the sidewalk and hit me.

This was just another example of how God protected me and kept me safe from danger. A witness who saw the accident from the doughnut shop across the street arrived and told the police that she saw me fly into the air and land on my back. Praise God, I actually had no real damage. They think the car was going about thirty miles per hour when it hit me. I had a throbbing headache and mild concussion from landing on the pavement, which lasted two weeks, but I had no scratches, fractures or broken limbs. I took eight hundred milligrams of pain killer for a couple of weeks, but after this experience it was becoming clearer to me by the day that God had His hand of protection on me.

I had always wanted to travel more when I was working as an operations specialist, so I ended up interviewing to become a flight attendant, my current profession. I left the stock market industry in August 1998 and moved to the Northeast, my first base posting with the airline. While there I met, dated and fell in love with Josh, a handsome, blue-eyed charmer who played with my emotions, so I used every opportunity to leave and return home and visit my mom who consoled me in the wake of his emotional abuse. It was during this time that my mother also confided in me letting me know that she had a daughter out of wedlock where circumstances forced her to give up the child for adoption. She wanted so much to find the child, so she embarked on a mission to find my sister through an ancestry search on the internet. The intimacy we shared was a bond that I think few mother and sons' have the privilege of sharing in this life. After all of life's experiences thus far, she had always been there, for her love was unconditional.

I received the biggest shock of my life in February 1999 when I received a call from my aunt Cora while on layover in Florida for work. She informed me that my mother, my best friend, died in her sleep at the young age of fifty-two years. I was hoping my mother would have been able to travel the entire world on my flight benefits, but that dream faded with the realization I would never see her again this side of heaven. Further, I realized that the only reason I became so utterly concerned about God's will, to the extent I did, was that she, my grandmother and great-grandmother were all instrumental in having prayed for, planted and nurtured that desire in me from a very young age. The Bible is clear that if you train up a child in the way he should go, and when he is old he will not depart from it (Proverbs 22: 6). Studies today even suggest that if you read the Bible to an infant, even though the child is not conscious of the words, seeds are being planted, and the child will grow up with a desire to seek God eventually.

The death of my mother made me realize that I needed God more than I ever had. My grandparents died in their fifties, and my great-grandmother died in her eighties; now that my mother had passed, I knew that I only had God left in my corner. I never had a relationship with my father, and my relationship to my dad's side of the family was minimal. During the probate of my mom's estate, I decided to revert to my mother's maternal surname in honor of her having been such a stellar, amazing mother. Since I never really cared for my first name, I also legally replaced my first name with my middle name. I knew that not having my father's surname going forward would be a non-issue, because I felt that my heavenly Father had always been present in my circumstances showing me that I didn't need to see myself through the eyes of the world. It was clear to me that God loved me and understood me better than anyone, so I decided to try to focus all of my attention on Him going forward by heeding what He was saying to me. I was always told that God's will was revealed in His scripture, so it was there that I knew I needed to seek answers about how to live correctly before Him.

Since I was seeking what direction my life should go after my mother's death, I decided to move back to San Francisco in

Chapter Five

the year 2000 which I thought would help me, while I administered her estate. I figured moving back home would also help me heal from the pain deep inside which resulted from Josh having broken up with me. I was now based and living in San Francisco which allowed me to drive home as needed to talk to attorneys and finalize my mother's business arrangements.

One nice early morning after reporting for work at the airport, I walked up to a departure gate, greeted the agent and asked him how his day was going. The agent said that everything was good except that the airplane which we were scheduled to fly on had just come in under an 'amber alert.' That term was not Inflight lingo, but I surmised that it must not have been a good thing. I asked what an amber alert was and he told me that it meant that in this particular instance, the plane's right engine had ingested a bird during takeoff out of Boston, but it was fixed, so all was well.

About ten steps later as I walked down the jet bridge, I felt a strong ache in the pit of my stomach, so I stopped as I wondered what it was. It was like no feeling I had ever felt before. It wasn't hunger pains or worry, but it was amazingly brief yet incredibly strong.

After standing a moment wondering, I continued to walk onto the airplane and began to complete my safety checks. I was the first flight attendant to board that outgoing flight that day, and I sat in the back at the furthermost second right door on the airplane. My colleague sat at the left door opposite me. We each had a window to view the outside area surrounding our respective door. We began takeoff roll and everything appeared normal, as it had many countless times before. However, approximately one minute after takeoff, the right engine blew, and it sounded like the engine exploded. It sounded like a bomb, the loudest boom I had ever heard in my life! The plane shook violently and it dove towards the ocean below. I recall praying a silent prayer saying, "Lord, if today is my day to meet You, then I am ready, Your will be done."

Simultaneously all electrical power went off, the ovens went off, and there was only darkness. My colleague to my left pointed to my window, clearly shaken as her beautiful, otherwise olive skin was pale and flushed. Since the window was above eye level, neither of us could see out of our respective windows, though we could each see across the aisle and out of the window of the other. She later told me she could see fire out of my window during the boom. The passengers were now all doing one of three things: screaming, crying or praying, and they were turning around, looking back to us for comfort. I just remember being at peace in my soul about dying, though my flesh was definitely shaken. My faith, years of expertise ignoring my emotional pain, a few years of flying and having studied the martial arts taught me to reflect a calm demeanor, regardless of what I was experiencing inside myself.

About fifteen minutes after the blast, gaining control of the airplane and climbing out of the dive, the captain made an announcement that the right engine had blown, and that we were dumping fuel in the ocean and returning to San Francisco International airport. He then informed the cabin that we needed to prepare for an emergency landing, for he didn't know the extent of the damage, thus continuing on to our destination was not an option. He directed the purser to have the flight attendants prepare the cabin for arrival in fifteen minutes. We landed safely, without incident, as we taxied to the gate with the left engine power only. We arrived without further incident, didn't have to evacuate slides, and upon deplaning, a nice passenger thanked us for taking care of them and for maintaining our professionalism, which allowed the customers to remain calm. I remember telling her that it was our training which prepared us, but her comment was so inspiring. She said, "I am a surgeon, and I operate in an operating theater." I told her that her job of protecting life had a higher degree of risk associated with it. But she continued and said, "Yes, but at least my operating room is never burning down around me. You as a flight attendant must

Chapter Five

do your job even though the aircraft might be disintegrating." I thought: *Wow, what wonderful insight.*

A few moments later, after all passengers deplaned, the captain debriefed us and said that in thirty years of flying, he had never experienced a situation like that, and I could tell that he was really scared. All of the female flight attendants started crying; I believe the stress of what just happened was beginning to sink in. I just recall saying, "Thank You, Lord, for keeping us safe." It was then that I realized the aching feeling in the pit of my stomach on the jet bridge was the Holy Spirit showing me that I needed to be vigilant, because something was about to happen.

I relate this story because it is just another example of how God has always been with me, showing me, guiding me and protecting me. Instances like this only continued to cement my belief that God was in complete control of what befell me in life, and that He was speaking to me always, and this experience was no different.

Simultaneously, I was growing in my martial arts prowess to such a degree that my instructor gave me an ancient Japanese name, the adopted name of a relatively unknown samurai in ancient Japan. This man, a Cameroonian by birth, worked aboard a European trade vessel, but he was recruited by Japan's then military leader, and he remained in Japan fighting and eventually dying as a personal retainer. Sensei felt I embodied some of the former samurai's martial qualities, so after I reached a level of proficiency, he invited me to participate in a special filmed by a major international network where I and a fellow classmate were shown displaying samurai sword skills at a park in San Francisco near Sensei's house. Sensei had written several articles about the Japanese sword over the years, and his connections due to his fame allowed him access to a variety of mediums wherein he could showcase his mastery of the Japanese martial arts. I didn't realize at first that God had masterfully orchestrated my path by allowing me to study the Japanese samurai sword. I knew over time that He would eventually show up and give me crystal clarity about how He had allowed all circumstances in my life to mold me into the image of who He wanted me to be.

CHAPTER SIX

A few years passed, and in 2004 I decided to leave San Francisco and move back East for a new experience. I felt that my life in San Francisco had run its course, for I wasn't meeting any guys I really liked. Additionally, my mother's passing made me realize that I needed to figure out which city I would call home. I began to look at the east coast for new base opportunities, and I decided to settle once again. I found a realtor online who picked me up from the hotel and showed me condos while I was on hotel layover. I had initially prayed and asked Father to allow me to buy a place, so I could avoid dealing with an apartment lease. It became clear after a few weeks that my desire to move and buy a place lined up with His will. Finding a godly realtor, choosing a condo and settling in just three short weeks were just more amazing examples of how God was meticulously ordering my steps. So, I packed up and moved to a new place where I embarked on a new chapter in my search for answers.

I call this timeframe stage three of my journey, since it was the time that I consciously started seeking God directly for an answer as to how I could live before Him, given that I saw myself as gay. This was also the year that I would first pick up the Bible and read it to completion.

I recall praying a prayer one night, asking God if I should continue serving as a flight attendant for a career. Later in the night, I had a wonderful vision of an angel visiting me in a moonlit garden. As I knelt to pray, she appeared by a tree, a beautiful, lithe, black woman in a long, flowing white gown, who told me that my job was exactly what I was meant to be doing. I learned over time that God spoke to me often in dreams, so it was there that I ended up getting lots of support from Him.

Since I had left San Francisco, I no longer was able to attend the church that I attended which was headed by a lesbian pastor. The pastor taught that the Bible verses dealing with sexuality were taken out of context by translators, so I had previously accepted her counsel as godly wisdom. After settling in the East again, I realized I needed a place to worship, so I started listening to sermons via radio, because I wasn't ready to find a new church home. The radio was easier for me during the transition of having left San Francisco. My questioning began, and I asked friends for their opinions about whether they thought homosexuality was okay with God or not. While listening to the radio, I started to hear lyrics in gospel songs that said homosexuality was not okay with God. I began to develop a newfound love for gospel music, but I made it a point to not include any gospel songs on my cell phone that spoke against homosexuality. The songs along with my internal struggle enabled me to finally summon the courage, as I realized that I had to stop guessing what God thought about homosexuality. So, I picked up the Bible and read it from beginning to end.

The women in my life had always taught me that God doesn't make mistakes, so naturally I felt that being gay was His will. The teachings upset what peace I did have, even though homosexuality was not preached about directly at this point. But, biblical teaching in general upset me, and I began to feel that similar pain inside of me that the Holy Spirit gave me on that jet bridge back in San Francisco. I had always felt that a minister must know better than me, right? Now that I had read the Bible, I was even more confused, because my former pastor in San Francisco said men had misinterpreted the Bible. So who was right? Yet now that I had read the Bible, my heart had become utterly convicted by what I read. The Bible is abundantly clear that scripture forbids homosexuality, not only in the Old Testament, but it is also condemned in the New Testament.

The main verses people tend to be familiar with that condemn homosexuality in the Old Testament are the following: Leviticus 18:22, 24-30 and Leviticus 20:13. The main verses noted in the New Testament are Romans 1: 18-32, 1 Corinthians 6: 9-11 and 1 Timothy 1:10. Of course there are myriad verses that deal with what God calls reprobate behavior, but these tend to be the most often cited.

I talked to gay friends who agreed with me and said that because the Bible was written by man, and man is imperfect, therefore scripture is imperfect. Deep down inside, though, I somehow knew that since I had finally read it, I knew I was without excuse if I ignored its precepts. As I continued to hear condemnation about homosexuality, my heart became more and more unsettled on the issue. That calm and peace that I had worked for years to build was now crashing down, and I was uncomfortable yet again inside myself. I somehow knew I may have been designed to be obedient to God, but how come I couldn't get there? So, the confusion continued, because these two notions were in conflict with each other inside of me. I wondered how could I as a gay person be obedient to God? I knew I could not in good conscience turn away from the pursuit of figuring this all out.

A month or so later, I was lying in bed with a guy I had met at a bar and had invited back to my apartment to have sex; there was no real date to speak of, we just wanted to have sex. Later in the day, after having had sex and falling asleep with him, I woke up in a cold sweat, terrified by a vision of my deceased grandmother. She pointed her right index finger into the middle of my forehead and said in an angry voice, "THAT'S NASTY!" I woke instantly, sat up in the bed, and knew that it wasn't a dream but a vision. I was so upset that I even told this stranger about the vision. I am sure he must have thought I was insane. She looked so angry; I knew it was real. The strange thing is that my grandmother, Laurentia, died over twenty-five years ago. At that time, I was barely twenty years old, still a virgin, not active sexually, and not even honest with myself about my sexuality, much less with anyone else. She certainly never had any knowledge of my sexuality, so why would my mind convey a message from her on this issue?

I now believe that God had allowed a representation of my grandmother to appear to me, because He knew I respected her authority and opinion. What I understood from the vision was that just because I had attraction to men, it didn't mean I could casually sleep with them. After the vision, I was still confused on the issue of homosexuality. Was God saying that the act of sleeping with a man I didn't love was unacceptable, or that being with a man sexually in any capacity was unacceptable? Being gay was such a big part of my existence up to this point, I felt that I couldn't walk away from being gay on a technicality or a guess. I still felt I needed a clearer, more direct answer, so the questioning continued.

I talked to many people on the left about the incident, as usual, and they said the vision was simply a representation of a lifetime of repressed guilt and that this experience had nothing to do with God. Somehow I knew better. This was my first of seven definitive interactions from God, and it was becoming clear to me that two men lying together was not okay with Him.

There are a couple of places in scripture, in Jeremiah for example, where God talks about sins of previous generations and how certain people engaged in various immoral practices, namely those of idol worship. Scripture is clear that God is a jealous God and will have no other gods before Him. God doesn't really give us all the reasons why it is detestable, but He alone sets the standard.

Jeremiah 32 is an example of how God is so displeased with the worship of idols that He even insists an entire city must be completely removed from the earth through destruction, and doing so also eradicates the behavior. He talks about how a city

Chapter Six

must be destroyed, its houses, altars, everything, but once the cleansing is complete He will return His people. I was still not sure conclusively that God was conveying this truth to me concerning homosexuality, so I continued to seek the heart of God on the matter, for I knew I needed absolute assurance.

It was now the summer of 2008, and I was still listening to the same minister who fed my soul often on Bible radio since 2004. One day he preached a sermon that veered into scriptural condemnation of homosexuality. I thought my life was going better. I had fallen back into complacency thinking that God didn't really care if I was gay, and then I heard this sermon. I believed that being gay was how God made me and that all I needed to do was be a good person. However, this sermon made me immediately uncomfortable, and I knew that this issue had to be settled once and for all. So I sent the minister an email, demanding he explain himself, and I let him know that it was because of people like him that gay people were committing suicide by slashing their own wrists and jumping off of bridges.

The minister's response to my email was to have one of his senior ministers, Cathleen, email me back. She responded in a loving, godly way, saying that the sermon was biblically sound, her lead minister was correct, and that I needed to face up to the fact that scripture doesn't distort or lie. It is truth, regardless of how painful it might be.

I was now at a point where I believed, regardless of how I felt, it was crucial to ask God what was the correct way to live before Him, especially when it concerned interpreting scripture. God Himself says that there are prophets who are false, so we have to speak to God about sensitive issues like this, so there is no confusion. I began to earnestly seek God yet again, because I had somehow believed that scripture was clear about sexual idolatry, but I needed to know conclusively how God viewed two men in a marriage, for example. Shortly after getting Cathleen's response and before going to sleep, I asked God to give me a vision much like the ones He had given Paul, Peter and other apostles in scripture, so I could finally understand what He wanted from me.

I believe we need to be careful about asking for signs, because scripture is clear that even though they are given signs, asking for a sign if one is an unbeliever is a rebellious act (Luke 11:29-32). By asking for revelation, we might also get an unexpected answer, and then what do we do with that information, especially if it is something we don't want to hear? So, after a few hours of sleep, I woke at three forty a.m., sweating, from a vivid vision. In the vision, I was talking with my brother, Jeff, outside on a sunny day in a non-specific, lush, green field. I remember in the vision that as I talked to my brother verbally, I asked God in my soul simultaneously, if it was okay to be gay and be in a committed, loving, monogamous relationship with another man. No sooner than getting the question out did black clouds, lightening, thunder, and rain appear, my brother was gone, and I was standing alone and terrified.

The turn of events terrified me, as all that remained were dark, turbulent skies above me, the trees and grass were gone, and in one swift motion, I was flying upwards, out of control, tumbling over and over toward the heavens. In the next instant, the rain, thunder and lightning were gone, the sun was shining, and I was flying along horizontally, completely at peace. I was wrapped in the palm of a hand, because I could feel the fingers against my ribcage. The fear and dread were gone, and what replaced them was a peace that truly surpassed understanding, exactly how scripture explained. I felt sheer joy and unconditional love, which was so strong that I wept, as I could not contain it. The skies were bright and sunny, and I knew I was in the palm of God's hand, as we flew slowly through the beautiful daytime sky. I could also see the shadow of giant wings on the clouds behind me, and to this day I don't know if they were God's wings or the wings of angels, for I never saw a body. However, there was no question that I was in God's direct presence.

I was so comfortable and content that I almost forgot why I had approached God in the first place. So, I asked Him again, saying, "Well, Lord, is it okay for me to be with a man or not?" No sooner had I asked the question than He dropped me, and I was falling this time, tumbling over and over towards the ground at break-neck speed. The feeling of unconditional love was replaced with a feeling of intense fear and inexplicable despair. Shortly before I hit the ground, I remember saying, "Okay, okay, Lord, okay, I will stop asking." Immediately I was standing upright again, the sky was sunny, my brother was back in front of me, his lips still moving, as though our conversation had never been interrupted. I was left with an indelible experience that had shaken me to my core. When I woke, I had a better idea that God might be telling me that He was not okay with homosexuality, but I was still not completely convinced. I prayed and thanked Him for the vision but deep down inside I was still unsettled.

Somehow, though I allowed the questioning to continue, because the truth was that I really didn't want to walk away from being gay. My common mistake after being shown truth was to invite those on the left to interpret the information. They maintained that God dropped me, because He was simply tired of me failing to understand that He made me the way I am. So, I decided to stick with that answer, because that was really the answer I wanted. So, that morning, I immediately sent an email to Cathleen, the associate minister who confirmed my fear that the dream meant God was displeased with homosexuality. She reminded me to keep in mind that God will never contradict scripture.

As uncertainty continued to replace what peace I had about being gay, I simply allowed the questioning to continue. I felt that I couldn't take a chance on misinterpreting this vision, and I couldn't leave it up to someone else to figure it out for me, either. Scripture says for one to work out his salvation in fear and trembling (Philippians 2:12). I was definitely doing that. Scripture is clear, though, that we are not to test God, and we need to be mindful at all times that His ways are not our ways. God is spirit and is under no obligation to respond how or when we request. I now know that He answers when He wants to, how He wants to, and if He wants to. I am so amazed at how He works. He is not man, so He won't respond the way a man might expect (Numbers 23:19). We may lack understanding at times, but if we trust and believe that He is God, then we know that whatever He does, He does for His glory and the good of those who love Him and are called according to His purpose (Romans 8:28). This was now my second vision from God on the topic of homosexuality and His clear direct view of it.

I put the matter aside and continued to convince myself that I was still not absolutely sure of what God was saying, so I continued to date men and told myself I would remain open to God for correction. It was now 2009, and I had taken a job transfer to experience and live in the Midwest. One night I had a vision of Christ putting His hand on the right side of my cheek, and I woke feeling completely loved and cherished. I could literally see His image slowly fade on the ceiling above me after waking. It was another powerful vision. The week before, I had told the Lord that I was going to attempt to be celibate, but my attempt to be celibate ended up lasting only about a week. I believe He was comforting me, knowing how hard it was for me to arrive at the decision to become celibate, but I still managed to remain confused about the issue. So, I continued to date men.

I also filed Chapter 7 bankruptcy for the second time, as I felt it was time to let the condo go into foreclosure that I had been renting out when I left The East. I had made several financial mistakes, and keeping the condo wasn't feasible, as the association dues topped four hundred dollars monthly. I knew I needed to consult the Lord about my decisions, but somehow I made a lot of decisions without clearly understanding His will regarding them. I allowed my brother to borrow thousands of dollars around this same time frame which put me in a financial tail spin; I felt that

Chapter Six

filing Chapter 7 bankruptcy for the second time in my life to be the correct course of action. I had mismanaged money for years, and I knew that at some point I would have to learn how to manage finances God's way.

Later that summer, I had the opportunity to work with a wonderful, godly woman. While working with her, I noticed that she kept mentioning scripture as she talked about God, thanked God for goings on in her life, and was simply a ray of light when it came to dealing with people. I had a feeling that she was a person who believed in a literal translation of the Bible, so I made it a point to keep the fact I was gay to myself, because I did not want to defend being gay with her.

Later in the day, she asked me, "Why do people feel the need to constantly come to me for guidance about their issues? Do I look like someone who wants to fix their problems?" I replied that maybe people viewed her as being closer to God than themselves, since she confessed God at every turn. Since she appeared to know God and His will, people maybe thought it was natural that she might have insight in helping them. She understood and thanked me for the reflection.

After work was finished, she asked me if I would like to join her for dinner at the local eatery, since we were on a layover and she didn't want to dine alone. Since we had a great working relationship and both loved the Lord, I said yes. At dinner, it was nice to be in a more relaxed, casual atmosphere. The conversation took a variety of turns, and at one point she became very quiet and contemplative and said that she was dealing with an issue she could not quite resolve. I told her to feel free to share, if she needed another person's viewpoint on the topic. Interestingly enough, she revealed to me that her daughter was lesbian. I braced immediately in an effort to prepare myself for the vitriol that would ensue, because I somehow felt she abhorred gayness, as she appeared to be very literal about scripture.

She said to me that she had a conversation with God on the topic. She said to God that she was so disgusted by her daughter's behavior that she had to shelve the issue, because she was too angry to deal with it. Then she told me that God's immediate reply to her was, "What about the sin you committed yesterday?" I was so blown away by the answer that I sat stunned and quiet, waiting for her to continue. Suddenly her mood became more solemn. She told me that she agreed with God, and in that moment, it was clear to me from this revelation that God was not even dealing with the gay issue at all. He was making it clear that we all have work to do in areas of our lives and no one is fit to judge except Him. It was then that I told her I was also gay and had struggled with the issue versus scriptural condemnation of it. She went on to say that she now believed that God allowed her daughter to be born gay as a test for her to learn to simply love gay people and not judge them. She believed that God allowed her to birth a daughter who was lesbian because this would force her to deal with and learn to eradicate her own homophobia.

This was an amazing revelation to me. It was such a humbling experience, that we both wept. I am even more awestruck about how God chooses to do things. This is not to say, however, that God abides sin. I am even finding that when someone is doing something wrong, and there is another party involved trying to help that person, then both of them usually have something to learn. They both in fact might be wrong about God's perspective, also. Having had this conversation with her, I believed God was also saying that her daughter didn't choose her orientation, but she had to learn to deal with her feelings and seek God for understanding.

Scripture says that God made them male and female (Mark 10:6); it does not say that we are born gay or straight. It also says that we are wonderfully and fearfully made (Psalm 139:14) and that it is not good for man to be alone (Genesis 2:18). The fact that God doesn't elaborate on other kinds of relationships other than male and female is that there is no other option acceptable to Him. I have decided that I will not add anything to scripture that is not there, and I will not take away from it anything that I don't agree with or dislike.

I said earlier in the book that I would explain why I believe people are born gay. I believe people are indeed born gay, but just because God allows it, that doesn't mean He did it. Some might be confused by this statement, but what I am coming to find is that the sin of Adam and Eve tainted all flesh. We all have a sin nature that needs to be reconciled to a holy God, and homosexuality just happens to be my persistent flaw. I actually believe it to be a curse passed down through the blood which is a direct result of the fall in the garden of Eden. He actually does say all other sin is outside the body. He says that a person engaged in sexual sin is sinning against his or her own body (1 Corinthians 6:18). I have often wondered about hermaphroditism, a condition that affects a very small percentage of people, but why did God allow them to be born that way? I also believe this condition to be one that is a result of the fall in the garden, since I don't believe that confusion of any kind is His will. Ultimately, I believe each person must go to God directly, so he or she can have peace in their soul. I believe these are issues which we must take directly to the Father to get clarification. God is clear in His word that He answers all prayer, if we pray according to His will when we ask (1 John 5:14-15).

I am coming to believe that scripture addresses any question we can fathom. Scripture says in Genesis that sin entered mankind through the fruit when Adam and Eve ate (Romans 5:12). God has been abundantly clear in scripture that homosexuality is not His design. I now am beginning to understand that every manner of sin in the world entered the world through that one defiant act of the first couple defying God's commands. God is clear that His thoughts are not our thoughts, nor are our ways His ways (Isaiah 55:8). We have to remember that He is spirit and we are flesh. If we try to reach God with our intellect, we will fail every time. We have to reach God with our hearts, for He is clear that we do not have a High Priest who cannot sympathize with our weaknesses, but was tempted as we are, yet without sin

(Hebrews 4:15). His word is clear that if we ask, it shall be given; seek and we will find; knock, and it will be opened (Matthew 7:7).

God loves us so much that He sent His Precious Son, Jesus to become flesh, that a fleshly body might be submitted for God to judge all sin on the cross, once and for all for all who believe (John 3:16). But, He is alive and well today, advocating for our needs (1 John 2:1). We also were crucified with Him on that cross (Galatians 2:20). If we accept the sacrifice, then we accept His gift. We can't reach Him, if we believe we are good or that we earned it. Christ is blameless, but He loves us so much that He chose to die in our place. All people on the earth are sinners in His eyes, because of the horrible sin of Adam and Eve, who ushered sin in by eating of the fruit. So, deep down inside, I believed that I had already received God's answer, though I was still not ready to accept it.

CHAPTER SEVEN

A few months after that incident, I met Shirley, another colleague who was going through some difficulties of her own in life. Shirley, a wonderful godly woman and I became friends after bonding on an issue close to her heart at work. She was going through a difficult circumstance, which was apparent to me by how she came across during our initial meeting. I felt it would be a very long day working with her, because she was combative, guarded and testy. I realized that I didn't need to interact with Shirley to do my job, so I consciously decided to work in the economy section of the airplane and leave her to take care of first class, since she was purser. However, later in the day I knew that I should talk to her, and I now recognize that feeling of knowing was the Holy Spirit directing me to talk to her.

As I mature in my relationship with the Lord, I have begun to recognize that when He speaks to me, He often chooses to show me His feelings on a matter through my emotions. I initially refused His gentle nudging about how I needed to talk to Shirley, for all I could think was that Shirley was no fun to be around, so why would I go talk to her? However, I knew that I needed to, so I relented, approached and asked how she was.

When I approached Shirley, she began to scurry about, and she showed me that she had extra food from lunch, and offered to feed me. I told her that I wasn't hungry; I simply came to ask how she was doing, since her manner was quite terse during our initial meeting. To my surprise, she immediately broke down into tears, and I felt awful. It turned out her mother was sick, her brother had become controlling about who would manage the bills surrounding her mother's illness, and it was causing her much stress. I somehow felt she knew the Lord, so I asked her and she replied that she did. I asked if she minded if we prayed, and she said no, so we prayed for the situation to be resolved at the behest of God's will.

The act of praying changed her mood immediately, and I knew that I had found a new friend. In discovering our mutual love for the Lord, we exchanged numbers, stayed in touch, and continued to encourage each other. We talked at length about how God simply loves us and wants us to do the best we can with what He gives us. She illustrated the point once by telling me of an experience she had with God. She told me that she was once lying in bed with her boyfriend, whom she was not married to, and God said to her, "Do you love him more than you love Me?" Of course, it was cause for immediate concern, so she started examining her heart, especially her relationship with both God and her boyfriend to find out what to do about it. She told me that after the initial question, some time had passed and she was lying in bed on a different occasion. She was talking to God in her heart while referring to her boyfriend, and God corrected her and called the boyfriend her husband. Again, she said, "my boyfriend," because she did not understand why God would call the guy her husband. She believed He corrected her, because in God's eyes, they were a married couple. I was talking to a colleague who is also a minister recently about sexuality, and he asked me if I knew when God considers a couple married. I told him that sure, when they take vows. His answer shocked me, when he said, no when the couple joins through sex. It is absolutely clear that God considers a couple married when they first have sex (Genesis 2:24). So in essence if a person is getting married for the first time, but he or she has had previous girlfriends or boyfriends they have slept with, then the person is actually an adulteress/adulterer if they are marrying someone other than the previous girlfriend or boyfriend!

I believe the revelation was simply that situations do not appear to us as they appear to God. I was remarking recently to a colleague how the Bible is clear that God views the beginning of the day as starting at sunset, when we view it as starting at sunrise (Genesis 1:5). Scripture has all the answers. In another instance, Tom, another work colleague, a minister who happens to be gay, told me his story about declining health and wealth, because his priorities were out of alignment with God's will for his life. When he rearranged and reprioritized his gay relationship in deference to God, then everything was restored. When he removed his boyfriend as being first in importance in his life and put God back in first place, everything reverted to normal. He said that even little things like saying good morning to his partner needed to be said after he had said good morning to God first. He also made an effort to get out of bed after a night's rest to read his Bible, before starting his day, and especially before having sex with his partner in the morning after waking. He told me that God simply wants to be first; He doesn't like second place. The gay issue is a non-issue, as long as it is not idolatrous, immoral, casual, and never first in one's life before a relationship with God, he believes.

The moral of both Shirley's and Tom's stories, for me at this point, was that God doesn't like second place and that He alone is qualified to judge. Tom's example, though, is not scriptural. God is clear that He rains on the just as well as the unjust (Matthew 5:45), so Tom could have still experienced blessing, even though he was living a life of disobedience.

God's word is simply and purely the truth. The Bible is real, it means what it says; it is not subjective (2 Timothy 3:16). God might in fact require very different behavior from two different people when both parties are dealing with an identical issue in life. He's sovereign; He can do as He pleases. We simply have to agree or disagree. He made life so very simple, yet we make it complex. The key for me now is to realize that whatever He says to me is truth, and I will be obedient to that truth to the best of my ability. I am learning that I don't have the strength or wisdom to answer all complex questions in life, but I know that we can do all things through Christ who strengthens us, just as scripture says (Philippians 4:13).

I now believe God views matters of sex and love as very serious. Some friends on the left and right have challenged me when I tell them of Shirley's example, saying that being unmarried is immoral and God would not tell her that He viewed her boyfriend suddenly as her husband. Scripture is clear that the marriage begins when the two lay together sexually. Those on the right would agree that Tom's example is not scriptural at all, because God would not okay two men being together sexually in any form.

I also know that scripture is abundantly clear that we will hear the voice of the enemy, or we will hear the voice of our fleshly nature, if we are not listening for or if we are not accustomed to hearing God's voice.

The Bible is very clear that people are deceived often by spirits, and the Bible is clear that satan is good at taking angelic form, because he used to be a creature of light (2 Corinthians 11:14). He is the master manipulator, so he can twist situations and make them appear to be the exact opposite of what they really are. I realize now, after finally reading the Bible, that we have to be on guard from deception, even if it comes in a way that makes us believe everything we are seeing and experiencing with our senses and emotions is real. The mind is the battlefield, and here is where the war takes place. Hell knows that we prefer to lean to our own understanding and that we figure out life through our own logic, but God says to guard against that.

It is becoming clear to me that we cannot rely solely on emotions, but we must rely solidly on the Bible and allow the Lord to use our emotions to show us the direction He has chosen for us. If we are scriptural with our foundation, then we will not be misled. It is the only truth. God is truth, therefore the Bible is the standard. Anything else is simply guessing. And this book is about my journey to truth, so I could never let it rest upon an assumption made by another human being. God made me, so it was to Him that I directed my pleas.

Friends on the left have been trying to convince me that God speaking to me about homosexuality was His attempt to help me learn to relax and simply live a good life as a gay man. Deep in my heart, though, I know that what He has said and shown me do not line up with that assumption. God knows what we are asking even before we ask it, so it would be naive of me to assume He didn't understand what I was asking when I requested the vision back in 2008. Scripture is also clear that God turns people over to certain behavior, if they desire said behavior strongly enough (Romans 1:28). He gave us free will, so we can do what we choose, but scripture is still clear about what is required for holiness. I realize that I may never get answers to certain questions in life, and that is okay, because I am finally reaching a point where all I care about is the fact that God is in control. So I am choosing to be obedient and trust Him implicitly.

I ran across a comment recently, by a pastor who said that we have an obligation as followers of Christ to know Him and to make Him known. How beautifully simple it really is. She believes we need to align our soul with our spirit, and that we are not here on earth to live either a purely spiritual or fleshly existence. We are to interface with a tangible world, so we have to learn to integrate our body, spirit and soul together. How that might look will depend on each respective individual who is examining his or her own life, and contrasting that with biblical truth. I know for my own understanding that I want to make sure that God's Spirit inside of me is the captain of my ship always, not my fleshly nature.

Shortly after the experience with Shirley, I met another wonderful woman on the airplane, a colleague, originally from Jamaica named Tamica, who is a Bible study teacher at her church. I asked her what she thought about homosexuality, and she said we could discuss it on the layover. So, we used our room keys and entered the conference room on our floor level in the hotel for a chat. Before we began talking, we prayed, asking God to guide us in Spirit and in truth. It was an intense conversation, and we both came to the same conclusion that the Bible is inerrant, but I still wasn't happy about what the Bible was saying, because I had so much invested in being gay.

Shortly into the discussion, someone tried to use his or her key to enter the room, and we could hear that the lock was not opening to let them in. I remarked how someone was trying to enter, and her reply was that this was a divine appointment, and the room was being blocked, for they were not meant to enter at that time. Shortly after we finished our talk and got up to leave the room, someone or possibly the same person from a few minutes earlier came and entered their key in the lock and this time it opened! She just looked at me and smiled. It was clear now they were welcome to enter the room, because the information that needed to be imparted had been given.

Cathleen, the minister who initially responded to me regarding the challenging letter I wrote to her senior minister about denouncing homosexuality is now one of my closest confidantes. Cathleen, who has become an amazing anchor in my journey, reminds me also that the words on the page, regardless of whether they were translated from Hebrew or Greek, are truth. The Holy Spirit recently intervened when I was witnessing to a colleague who used the argument that man wrote the Bible, so it is not the word of God. The Holy Spirit gave me an analogy in my spirit to share with my coworker that even floored me. I felt the Father directing me to ask my colleague if he believed whether the Virgin Mary was human. I then was led to ask if he believed the men who wrote scripture were human. The coworker's answers were both yes. I was then directed to tell him that the Holy Spirit overshadowed both Mary and the writers of the Bible in similar fashion, and they each bore the word but in different forms. In Mary's case, Jesus was born, and the word took on flesh. In the case of the writers of the Bible, Jesus was inscribed on the page, and He became the Holy Bible. It is a matter of form, but He was born just the same! I have to say my coworker was awed, as was I. It pretty much stopped his line of questioning in its tracks.

So, whenever questioning the word, we need to ask the Holy Spirit to teach us, for He will reveal all truth (John 16:13). I have recently begun asking God to soften my heart, so I can understand more truth. I now ask for the courage to obey the truth, as well as to have it revealed to me. And I ask for the courage to navigate said course, even if I don't like or understand the motivation behind it. The key for me is obeisance. I won't lean to my own understanding, but I will remain open to what God says about an issue. Shirley knew very well what I was going through with regard to my struggle to understand God's will about sexuality, so I wanted her to understand what God had told me and no longer rely on guesswork.

CHAPTER EIGHT

A year or so later during the summer of 2010 I moved to Europe for work. I rented a room in a small flat from a wonderfully sweet believer named Mita who lived with her youngest son, Newsom. She also rented my colleague, Dennis a room in the flat, and it was good to be in a house with love all around me. Mita and I had constant dialogue about the Lord, and I marveled at her faith in Him. I lived with Mita for six months, then I moved into my own studio flat in an orthodox Jewish enclave in my city. During this time Shirley kept me in prayer that I would find peace, for I was still not understanding or wasn't willing to heed God's truth about homosexuality through His visions to me completely. One day I arrived in the U.S. from Europe, and I reported to my hotel after the work day ended. When I turned on the television in the room, to my amazement, a minister was in a pulpit preaching a sermon condemning homosexual behavior. It was a weekday about four p.m., and here I was turning on the television without even having turned the channel! Usually the television comes on with the menu channel playing, but in this instance, God had clearly orchestrated the sermon.

   I continued to struggle yet again, because I just wasn't ready to understand. I wondered, was He saying to me, "Look at this minister preaching a message of hate, for that is not Me, but man"? Or was He saying, "This minister is correct; the gay lifestyle is incompatible with Christian life"? Often times, people on the left would say that the scriptures dealing with sexuality are in the Old Testament and that we are now under the New Testament, so the old law does not apply. Yet I have found that view to be only partly true. I understand that we are now under the New Testament according to Christ, Himself. But not only are there rules in the New Testament dealing with sexual mores, they are even expanded and even more detailed than those of the Old Testament.

Christ also was clear when He said that He came to fulfill the law, not to annul it (Matthew 5:17). So, the old testament does apply to the modern believer, but we just have to know how to rightly divide the word of truth. I heard a minister recently say that the Old Testament is unfolded in the New Testament, and the New Testament was hidden in the Old Testament. I believe God is clearly saying that He loves all of His children so very much, but living our lives only according to feelings without listening for His voice is not how we can navigate life. Obedience to His will is more important than what we think. However, I was still not ready to relinquish this part of me that I had worked so hard to build.

So, immediately after the sermon on television, I called my friend Shirley and related to her that I needed help getting to the truth, for I was completely dismayed. I cried out to God in tears, asking what He wanted from me. Shirley told me to stop what I was doing, and she invited me to pray with her on the phone. She prayed a direct, clear prayer on the phone with me, asking God to settle my heart and to let me know in a loud, clear voice that it was okay to be in a committed, loving, monogamous, gay relationship, so I would finally be at peace about the issue.

After she prayed, I felt an immediate peace come over my soul, as the issue had again been submitted to the Father for clarification. I love feeling the presence of God in my soul, and I know that where two or more are gathered in His name, there He is also. So, that very next night after returning home, I was sitting on the edge of my bed having the normal mind chatter with myself about my day, reminding myself that I had to pick up dry cleaning and groceries the next day. I remember saying to myself, without even being conscious of it, "God, please settle my heart", when He immediately, loudly and clearly interrupted my train of thought. He didn't even let me finish the thought.

The only words I could get out in my mind were, "God, please settle..." and then a sound like a rushing wind invaded my mind and forcibly blew all of my thoughts out of my mind. My head became completely clear and quiet. It felt like a sword had cut my thoughts in half vertically, and the force of the sword was a mighty wind that blew my thoughts out of my head instantly. Just a second or so later, as though standing at my right shoulder, I heard God speak loudly and clearly into my right ear, "IT'S ALREADY SETTLED!"

It became abundantly clear to me now that God realized He needed to speak to me exactly as Shirley had prayed for, and I now realize that He meant for me to shelve this issue once and for all. I remember trembling for a moment after, because upon hearing His voice, I lost all composure. I remember thinking that I would have loved to have hidden under a table. I immediately praised Him and thanked Him for talking to me and for not destroying me, because I certainly had struggled over the years and asked Him plenty of times for clarification on this issue.

I now understand a little bit of what people in scripture must have felt when an angel of God appeared to them. My experience was only a voice, so I cannot imagine what I would feel if an angel appeared to me directly. I now know why angels always say "Fear not." God is truly all powerful, after all, so one will definitely tremble when He approaches. Anyway, my fear was replaced with a calmness of spirit, peace, and love upon Him speaking to me. There was no confusion, only joy. Interestingly enough, I still wasn't completely sure if He was saying it was not okay to have a gay relationship.

So, why did doubt remain? I knew He was saying the issue was settled, but did that mean the question of my desire being normal

Chapter Eight

was settled in the fact that He made me and He doesn't make mistakes? Or did it mean that His disapproval of the gay lifestyle was documented and settled in scripture? I continued to doubt and remained willfully disobedient, I have to say, because deep down inside I believed it was not okay to be gay, yet I couldn't find the strength or the courage to walk away from my desires. After all, I had been that way since I could remember. I actively started dating men at twenty-one years old, and I was now forty-two years old, so the pattern of denial had been firmly established.

God will never contradict His word, so I was misunderstanding Him by agreeing with Shirley, for I needed to finally accept the truth of His word. I called Shirley and shared with her my findings and she rejoiced at the outcome. We both assumed He was saying that I could now live in peace and find a man to love. However, I surmised over time that just because God agreed to answer Shirley's prayer, it didn't mean He was agreeing with what she was asking for. Upon further reflection, it is clear to me that the issue of two same gender loving people is not God's will ever.

This was the first time He spoke audible words to me while I was awake, but His choice to speak out loud to me gave me a clear answer about His heart as it regards homosexuality. This is what I was really looking to find, a definitive line drawn in the sand, so I could rest on the topic of sexuality.

During the same time Shirley prayed with me while on layover, I had been dating a handsome guy named Eiven who lived near Wales. He told me on our first date that he was an atheist. When he admitted that, I immediately asked God: was I supposed to walk away from him, or was I put in his path, so he could learn that God was real? I wasn't sure about the answer, so I simply continued dating him. We dated for eight months, and I really thought I was going to marry him and remain in Europe for the rest of my life, since gay marriage was already legal there, but I somehow knew inside that God had other plans. I met him on a gay date site the first month of living in Europe after having moved in with

Mita. Eiven lived a two-hour train ride north of me, and we would see each other only on weekends.

One weekend, the long holiday, Queen's Day, he invited me to his house to spend the weekend, and I was eager to go. After going shopping locally where he lived, we cooked and made dinner. Later that night, we finally lay down to sleep. About three a.m., I woke up gasping, couldn't breathe and knew immediately that I was having an asthma attack. Unfortunately, I had left my asthma inhaler at home. Since it was Friday night, and it was Queen's day on Monday, there would be no store open in the morning where I could buy a new inhaler. Eiven had to take me immediately Saturday morning to the clinic where I would get a new inhaler.

Later that second night, Saturday, again about three a.m., I woke up having another asthma attack, so I took my inhaler and used it, but it didn't work! Somehow I knew that when the medicine wasn't working, God Himself had blocked the medicine's path. I somehow knew this, though I couldn't explain why. I now believe it was because God had given me ample warning about His will regarding homosexuality, and He was growing tired of me denying His word. So, I told Eiven I believed God Himself was orchestrating this, and I made it clear that we had to call off the relationship. It broke both of our hearts, but I knew it was the right thing to do. So, I took the train back home on Sunday morning, but Eiven and I stayed in contact. I was in the process of moving to a new apartment around this time, so deep down I think Eiven thought that once I got settled, having left my then roommate situation that I would be able to find the peace to see clearly and continue dating him. But I knew better.

During this same time frame, I started to break out in boils from head to toe. I had them in my nose, on my face, in my ears, on my arms and legs, and on my posterior. I went to the medical clinic and they diagnosed me as having Methicillin-resistant Staphylococcus aureus (MRSA). I was also itching from head to toe a couple of weeks during this same time frame, and the doctor could find no reason why. It felt as if I had body lice, since I had them once in college, having picked them up from a contaminated bed, but I had not been in a situation that would explain being exposed to them this time. Also, I was having a bloody anal discharge that would last days. One time I was sitting on my computer chair, and when I rose to grab tea, the seat was soaked in blood. I believe each medical experience that came upon me was punishment for my willful disobedience of ignoring Father's warnings that homosexuality was not His will for my life. I had decided not to marry Eiven, but I continued to date men somehow thinking that I would find peace, if I chose a different partner. Maybe I didn't have peace, because Eiven was atheist I told myself. But deep down I really knew why I didn't have peace. I am reminded by the example of Job in scripture and how God allowed boils to befall him, as the devil attacked him in an effort to embarrass God. My situation was interestingly similar.

CHAPTER NINE

About a year or so later, my view on God's will about homosexuality continued to evolve, and I felt He had been sufficiently clear with me about His feelings. However, sadly, over time I began to fall back into dating men. I wanted to be obedient, but I simply lacked resolve. I struggled yet again and continued to date men, and conviction unsettled my heart yet again. I realize now that God simply would not let me rest. He had brought me too far to give up on me, for He had originally orchestrated a divine plan for me even before I was formed in the womb, though He knew I would disobey Him and follow the lusts of my fleshly nature.

I moved back to the East coast in February of 2012, because I was finding Europe to be too expensive, I wanted custom samurai swords made, and I also knew that getting married and staying there would not be in line with what God had been revealing to me. Since I would not be marrying a man, my legal status would not allow me to stay beyond my three-and-a-half-year visa restriction, and I would have to return anyway. So, I rented a room from Derek, a good friend of mine, while I saved money and paid off bills. My dad died a few months after I returned to which corresponded with my custom-made samurai swords arriving as well. I also formally stopped kenjutsu class in San Francisco, since Sensei had stopped practicing combat training and was instead focused only on 'kata' or technique training. I

Chapter Nine

had learned to perform kata perfectly on my own, but I needed a sparring partner in order to continue the combat exercises. My life had been moving me eastward for quite some time, and I believe the Lord was allowing me to come back to the U.S. in part, because it would be easier handling my dad's effects, just as I had handled my mother's effects while living in San Francisco. This was my third time living on the East coast, and I began to date a wonderful Irish diplomat whom I met online. I started dating men again, because I told myself I was unclear what God had been communicating to me.

Right around the time I was dating him, I received another vision while I was sleeping in my rented room. I realize now that I am always so happy and elated to hear God's voice in visions, that my soul leaps for joy and it cannot be contained. This alone convinces me that I love Him, and that I am His forever. This time He said, simply, "Stuart..." And I replied, "Yes, Father" (looking up to heaven, being so happy to hear from Him again). He continued and said, "If that is what you are going to do, then it needs to be loving, committed, and monogamous."

When I woke the next morning, I thought it was so great that He had changed His mind on the issue. But why now? After examining the Bible and talking with my big sister, Cathleen, the minister, it became shockingly clear that the vision was not from God but satan. Cathleen and I only talk via email, but this time she felt it necessary to call and see how I was doing walking away from homosexuality. She made sure that I understood finally that God is not the author of confusion (1 Corinthians 14:33); His word is abundantly clear. It was now becoming clear that the final vision was from the devil or a demon masquerading as God in an attempt to keep me in confusion! This is exactly how he tricked Eve when he said, "Did God really say you couldn't eat of the tree of the knowledge of good and evil?" Whenever the devil interjects a question, his aim is always to pull us off balance and get us to question the truth. The battlefield is the mind, so we have to learn to guard our minds against the wiles of the enemy.

We have to ask for the entire armor of God to cover us, so we can withstand the enemy's attacks (Ephesians 6:10-18).

I am now clear that when He said the issue was settled He meant that He was also finished talking to me about the issue. If I wanted to continue to delude myself with a lie, I believe He would allow the enemy to have me after all. The Bible says that He will turn us over to sin, if we persist so. The apostle Paul talked clearly about the topic of homosexuality as an affliction that affected many believers, but they were washed and made clean (1 Corinthians 6:11).

I believe we have to remember that there is a battle taking place for our very souls, and we have to remain on guard at all times. Someone on the left might say that I am mistaken and that God changed His mind on the homosexual issue in reference to my visions and Him speaking, but I am abundantly clear that He never changes His mind about issues of morality. Would He suddenly say that adultery is okay, as long as all parties involved vowed to only do it one time? No, the answer is a definite no. A person on the left might say that they are still unconvinced that being gay is not okay with God. I would then urge that person to approach the Father, and read His word just as I have. What He showed and told me has changed me forever.

The beautiful thing is that God allowed me to roam for years before I finally decided to agree with Him, and He still decided to cover and protect me that entire time! He is so patient and loving. I don't claim to have all of the answers about homosexuality, but I definitely believe that He is clear in His word, and He was clear with me that same gender love is not His will for His children. The Bible is clear that God doesn't give us a spirit of fear either, but of power, love, and of a sound mind (2 Timothy 1:7).

God has been so amazing in showing me favor throughout my life that it feels so good to be able to notice His handiwork all around me more and more. While living on the East coast this third time around and renting the room from my friend, Derek, I knew that living with someone who didn't espouse my beliefs might be difficult. Derek is Jewish, and he doesn't believe Christ is the Messiah. But, I believe God has given me a heart for Jewish people, and I am now beginning to see that our friendship also is an opportunity for him to see that God is real and that Jesus is God in the flesh. Upon moving in, I knew I would need use of a car until I would be able to buy one, so we agreed I would use his spare car, a Volkswagen Jetta, until I was able to save enough money to buy my own car. I gave him enough rent money to cover both the cost of the room and the use of a car. It really was a great car, he bought it brand new, it had never had any problems, it was the top of the line, and he took amazing care of it. While driving it, I started to really like it, so I asked Derek if he would be willing to sell it to me. At first he said no, but eventually he came around and agreed that I could buy it, if I wanted. Upon him saying yes, I decided to ask God for a sign if the car was for me or not.

Miraculously enough, almost a week after asking God for advice, the car starting leaking anti-freeze. A friend called me and told me to check the radiator, because the car had leaked fluid in his driveway. I told Derek, so he took the car in to Volkswagen to have it serviced and fixed. Approximately two weeks after that incident, I was driving a colleague to my house when the air conditioning fan blew, the car stalled, and smoke came out of the air vent inside the car. So, Derek took the car in again, and it needed to have circuits replaced, as they were fried. It ended up costing about three thousand dollars. Finally, I came home from a trip overseas and got into the car, which had been sitting for four days, and when I tried to start the car, it wouldn't start! Again, here was not only one sign but three! This was becoming laughable, and upon taking it in, it turned out that the car needed a new battery. Derek asked me what kind of a curse I put on his car, to which I replied, "All I did was pray for an answer as to whether the car was for me or not. I definitely have my answer, so I won't be able to buy it, sorry." This was just another example of how God has kept me all of my life, always showing me favor and taking care of my needs.

Similarly, about a month later, I decided that I wanted to buy a 2004 Nissan Maxima. I found one in a want advertisement, and I drove the Jetta out there to test drive the used Maxima. The owner let me take it to Nissan for an inspection before I bought it, and I found out it had a laundry list of things that were wrong with it. So I took it back to the owner and made him promise not to sell the car, unless he revealed to the prospective buyer what was wrong with it.

Before I left the lot to return the car to the owner, I felt God directing me to ask the dealer if they had another car on the lot that was for sale. I am really beginning to notice the feeling inside of me as being from God, so I asked if they might have something in my price range. It turned out they had a 2001 Infiniti I30 that belonged to an older man who died and left the car to his son, who then sold it to the dealership. Upon test driving the car, I had a tremendous peace and somehow knew this would be my car. I returned the Maxima to the owner, and I drove the Jetta back to the dealership to complete paperwork. Then a guy with whom I had gone on a few dates gave me a ride to the dealership the next day, and I picked up the car that I would now drive to and from work. It was a great car in amazing condition with low miles, and I was getting used to it. One night, however, after having driven home from a long day at work, I was pulling away from a stop light, when a van careened into the back of my bumper totaling the car!

It was a blessing that I wasn't seriously hurt. I had slight pain in my left arm and neck, but that went away in a few hours. Funny enough, I started to look at Infinities on the Infiniti website, since I had been driving one previously. I wasn't sure I could afford another one, because they were definitely not cheap cars. But again, I know God directed me to look at the website, as I was becoming more familiar with His voice. Upon looking at the site, I came across a 2004 I35, the replacement model for the

Chapter Nine

one that had just been wrecked. It had a bigger engine, bigger wheels, more leather; in essence it was a little more luxurious. It was quite a bit more money than the 2001 had cost, so I wasn't sure if I could afford it.

Still, I kept looking at the website for a few days, and since it hadn't been sold, I felt that God was holding that car for me. So, I went to the dealership and inquired about it, test drove it, and applied for the loan. Wouldn't you know I was approved? It was amazing, and I drove off of the lot with pretty much the same car that had been wrecked previously, though this was much better, and it was simply beautiful. This car experience was just another in a line of many where God showed up and blessed me beyond what I had expected. He has continually shown me favor in my life, and I promised myself long ago that I would always seek His face for everything that concerns my heart.

So no matter what comes, I know God is intimately concerned about my life and how I respond to the situations that present themselves. Sexuality is just another area of my life where I desire His peace, so I owe it to myself to be obedient to what He shows me.

In February of 2014 I transferred my job to the Southwest, since living expenses there are cheaper than the East coast. I wanted to position myself in order to make godly financial choices for the future. The fact that my dad lived there also made moving there desirable, so I could administer his estate locally. I had made a lot of financial mistakes up until this time, and I now understand that being in debt is not the will of God. Buying the Infiniti along with custom-made samurai swords costing twenty-five thousand dollars plunged me into a mess I needed to get out of as soon as possible, if I was going to focus on building a life with a firm spiritual foundation for the future.

Since 1990 I was able to collect, buy, and sell many more swords, but over the years I lost most of the money my mother left me from her estate through foolish purchases on swords. God recently helped me to see that the swords are an idol. I would be sitting worshipping Him and a sword would appear in my spirit and would manifest as a picture in my head during worship. I had to consciously concentrate hard to make it go away. Even here the Holy Spirit was showing me that I had an improper relationship to said item. He is even showing me that martial arts have a spiritual component, and even though they are used for protection, since the desire to protect myself was itself an act of violence, thus I was in error. He has made me see clearly that He alone is my protection, for I don't need to protect myself. He has also shown me that I am still indeed samurai, because samurai in Japanese means 'to serve'. But, instead of wielding a razor sharp samurai sword, I have picked up the Bible which says that it too is like a sword, double-edged to be exact. God says, "for the word of God is living and powerful, and sharper than any two-edged sword, piercing even to the division of soul and spirit, and of joints and marrow, and is a discerner of the thoughts and intents of the heart" (Hebrews 4:12). So, I am no longer serving my own fleshly desires; I am serving my Lord and Savior in completing His work. I am learning to trust Him in all things. In an effort to be obedient to Him, I sent my swords, my collection of samurai films, and all my samurai collectibles to a consignment shop in Chicago, for I wanted to be firmly rooted in God's unadulterated will.

Ultimately, I know the Lord allowed me to go to the Southwest where I rented a room from a work colleague, so I could continue paying off debt, administering my dad's estate and reconciling my sexuality in order to be firmly rooted in all truth, as He positioned me for where He would direct me next.

I now understand that God wants to be included in every decision we make, for He delights in being in relationship with us completely. He now had effectively communicated to me that He alone is all I need, and defining myself as gay and as a martial artist needed to change. I now no longer make decisions without consulting God, for my heart is very concerned with consulting Him before I make a decision about something. It has become clear that He even required I sell the swords, the things I prized most in the world. For scripture is clear where your money is, your heart is there also (Luke 12:34).

It is now clear to me that God used and continues to use all of my life's experiences to get me to a place where I can carry the good news of Jesus to others who are trapped in a belief that says homosexuality is God's will for their lives. *My move to the Southwest corresponded with my heart truly cracking open before God; I am now abundantly clear God has always required that I walk away from homosexuality from the beginning.* I am now on fire for the Lord, and I know what He means in scripture when He says that He would rather we be hot or cold, for if we are lukewarm, He will spit us out of His mouth (revelation 3:16). We must understand how to rightly divide the word of truth; we must not mix law and grace. We must understand that truth is not contingent upon how we feel. I realize that choosing to totally believe His word was a process that took many years. But, I know it happened in totality with the move to the Southwest. I think I also partially understand how it must have felt to have been a Sadducee or Pharisee thousands of years ago. To reject Christ, but to somehow still believe one is doing His will is definitely a contradiction, and many are deceived all the while, thinking that God is pleased with choices they make. It is one thing to suspect something, but it is quite another to have truth revealed and believe it.

I had always known that I was born again and saved from the possibility of going to hell upon dying since having gotten baptized during my teenage years. It was then that I confessed Christ as Lord and believed in my heart that I wanted to live for Him. Looking back, I can say that having a reborn spirit didn't make me feel any different than when I had a dead spirit, but the Bible is clear that feelings don't indicate what is true. The Bible says that becoming born again is a manifold process. Justification refers to position, as God views the person as being righteous and covered under the blood of Jesus. Sanctification happens simultaneously which refers to one's condition, as the sin is cleansed. At this point one is no longer viewed as being a sinner in God's eyes. Jesus' blood excised and paid for all past, present and future sin on that person's account upon belief and confession of the individual. Also, God gives the person His Spirit, so the person is now indwelling a perfect spirit which is the same spirit that Jesus has. Jesus addressed this issue perfectly in scripture when Jesus answered, "most assuredly, I say to you, unless one is born of water and the Spirit, he cannot enter the kingdom of God" (John 3:5). He is confirming the fact that the person in fact has now become clothed with the righteousness of Jesus and not of his or her own. We were first born from flesh (water), as we left the womb, but the new birth happens in the spiritual realm which denotes our new and true nature. Sanctification is also a continual process which identifies and eradicates the effects of sin over the remainder of the person's natural life, as God transforms the person's mind to match the perfect spirit living inside of him or her through the reading, studying and ingesting of the Bible. As one believes the Bible and allows the Holy Spirit to change him or her from the inside out, he or she will eventually reach a point at the end of life where the presence of sin is completely removed. This process continues and one will eventually reach the place where his or her physical body is transformed into a spiritual body upon the return of Jesus; this is called glorification.

I maintain that I never had peace about being gay, because I believe the Holy Spirit inside of me convicted me that homosexuality was wrong the instant I became born again. Had I chosen to remain in gay relationships after being reborn, I would never have found peace, because the conviction of the Holy Spirit would never let me remain in a sinful state and be okay with it. I now know that God wanted me to gain deeper understanding about the entire process of truly becoming His adopted son, so I could finally experience what living a life that pleased Him was really like. This was the turning point, when my spiritual eyes were opened. I felt that God was saying to me that when He spoke to me in Europe, He spoke into my ear and not in my heart, because at that time my heart was not His. I was indwelling the Holy Spirit, since I believed when I was baptized in my youth. However, since I came to love the sin of homosexuality more than God, my heart grew hard to Him, and I was not able to hear His voice clearly. The moment I confessed to Him that I believed His word and wouldn't compromise it any longer corresponded with hearing His voice inside my spirit during the move to the Southwest in February 2014.

He is beginning to put crystal clear thoughts and images inside my spirit, which manifest in my mind when He speaks to me. I began to feel that if I continued on my present course I would indeed find myself so hardened to the truth, I would not be able to see my way clear. I could eventually find myself being turned over permanently to a reprobate mind and left to my own devices. We are now living in a time when some will depart from the faith, giving heed to deceiving spirits and doctrines of demons (1 Timothy 4:1). We don't get to determine if a course we are on is holy, that is God's privilege. We simply have to agree or disagree with what He says.

I am sharing my journey, my story, because it is really God's story. He loves us so much that He wants all of us to live in a way that glorifies Him. Also, nothing happens on His watch without His notice. God is still on the throne. He is the same God, today, yesterday and forever. He never changes His mind about morality. A friend of mine believes that God changes His mind on issues. But, my friend fails to understand that when God changes His mind, it is never a matter of morality. He might change His mind about the time frame that a particular trial should endure, for example, but the time frame of a trial, for example is subjective. His truth is not subjective. A good example is the story of King Hezekiah, who asked God if he could have years added to his life after God had told him he was initially going to die. God relented and added fifteen years to his life (Isaiah 38:5). God relented and added years to his life, but I had to help my friend understand that God changing His mind about a situation is never a change of mind about His morality. I know it is a difficult pill to swallow, but trust me when I tell you that no gay man wanted a husband more than I did.

When I got to the Southwest, I could tell I was becoming a new creature. After moving, I immediately called Ted, a guy I had gone on a date with while there on vacation, as I was checking out the city in anticipation of moving there. Ted is Catholic and believes that it is okay to be gay, so we did not see eye to eye about homosexuality. He still goes to mass, but he prefers to believe that I am wrong about this issue. I had to walk away from dating him as well as all other men, when I made the decision to believe God completely. My journey has not been an easy one at all for others to accept. Most of my friends who I thought were friends have simply walked away. A former close gay friend of mine was very angry with me and said, "So, what, are you straight now?" I told him that I am simply clear what is right and what is wrong. I told him also that I believe that the opposite of homosexuality is not heterosexuality, but holiness. I am starting to make new friends, and I am meeting many, many colleagues who as believers are also coming into closer, tighter personal relationships with Jesus. This is encouraging, because I believe God is allowing me to take this journey, because He loves me dearly. I know He wants me to understand that He died for my freedom and that He wants me to live a victorious life in Christ Jesus.

CHAPTER TEN

As I continue to be sanctified, the desires of the old man, my old dead spirit, continue to come up. I recently had a dream wherein I pushed a man who was pursuing me into a room filled with flame that then consumed him. A work colleague, Kylie who happens to be a minister told me that the person in the dream being pushed into the fire was the old man being dispatched by the new man. She maintains that as the new man got stronger, he was able to push the old man into the fire which signified the death of homosexual desire. My fleshly nature remembers old behaviors and my body is quick to remind me of past behavior in dreams. The area that I believe to be the most difficult to conquer has been that of masturbation. Even though I walked away from the bookstores, bathhouses, pornography, nightclubs, dating, online sites, and parties, the desire to masturbate never went away. I believe that this is an area where sanctification will simply extinguish the desire in time. I believe sanctification extinguishes all ungodliness. I have been struggling a lot in this area lately, because I realize just as I yielded and agreed with God about homosexuality, this issue is bigger than me. It requires an effort that I know I cannot muster on my own. Just like God delivered me from prescription anxiety medication and sexual promiscuity years ago, I know He will deliver me from the desire to masturbate, also.

I even found myself asking friends for advice again, a practice I know is never ideal, especially if the person doesn't believe the Bible. God says to not seek the counsel of the ungodly (Psalm 1:1). Scripture doesn't use the word masturbation in the Bible, but Christ was abundantly clear that to use the body, the temple of the Holy Spirit, in a way that fulfills a lustful desire is indeed sin. God knows I have been struggling with the issue, and while I was recently walking in the parking lot of my job after a long trip, God spoke to me about masturbation. He knew I was somehow trying to rationalize that masturbation was okay, since I was not lying with another man. Yet deep inside, I knew that to be false. Christ was clear that if we lust after a person in our mind, then the sin has already been committed (Matthew 5:28). An acquaintance who also walked away from being gay thinks that masturbation is okay, because he views it as being massage. But, if one is really honest, he will see that masturbation requires a thought of something or someone to fuel the passion that leads to the act. When I walked through the parking lot at work, it was a dark, clear night and three words popped directly into my spirit and were plastered in my head. He said, "MASTURBATION IS ADULTERY!" I stopped dead in my tracks, looked up to the star-filled sky and said, "Okay, Lord, yes, I understand." I would now caution my friend to read 1 Corinthians 3:17, for we cannot defile the temple (body).

I am now becoming clearer daily that everything in my life has been pushing me towards developing a closer relationship with my Lord and Savior Jesus Christ. God choosing to speak to me about masturbation was just another example of how He feels about morality. Even though the words He used are not those exactly written in scripture, His message to me shows how He is present, listening, and cares about everything that concerns my heart, even to the point of tailor making an answer for me, so I could understand Him completely. The fact He spoke to me in the parking lot was tailor made, because He knew I would immediately understand. I now can see that God is allowing the thorn

Chapter Ten

of homosexuality to pull me towards Him instead of pushing me away from Him. The devil now tries to use my old thoughts of past relationships to tempt me into masturbation, but I know it is a trap. So I pick up my Bible and read, or I simply pray and the urges flee. I am now sufficiently clear that one can't have a testimony without going through a test. Interestingly enough, every time I got to a place where I understood the word to be true and believed it, a peace came over me that was amazing. My fleshly nature found this difficult, since it wanted to be with a man, but I now understand why spirit, soul and flesh are in direct opposition to each other.

If the spirit is dead, then the soul is easily lulled and pulled by the fleshly nature. However, when the spirit is born again, the fleshly nature and the spirit truly become oil and water. The soul then becomes the bounty that must be conformed to the likeness of the new spirit by the renewing of the mind, as on one reads scripture. Regardless of whether we like to hear it or not, truth is truth. God spoke to me in a night vision that summer and said to me repeatedly "READ DEUTERONOMY 4:2." Upon waking I remembered that the Lord had visited me in the night, telling me to read His word. As I opened my Bible to Deuteronomy 4:2, I was reminded that I was never to add or take away from scripture. Accepting this reality led me to a place where I have finally found complete joy in trusting and believing God at His word. My friend, Cathleen, also asserts that God will never allow us to be tempted or test us beyond what we can bear (1 Corinthians 10:13). He loves us so much that He is willing to let us roam and figure things out even if we aren't seeking Him.

In finally reaching the point where I now believe that the Bible is completely true, I realize it has taken all of my trials to bring me to this new reality. It took my whole life really to get to this point. I was actually quite disappointed with myself when I was fooled by the last vision before leaving the East coast, wherein I was deceived into thinking that the demon that spoke to me in the vision was God. I wondered: how could I be misled?

I believe I was influenced by the demonic spirit in the last vision, because deep down inside I really still desired a male partner. I have come to understand that accepting Christ in my heart and confessing He is Lord is what saved me from hell, but true repentance, turning from my previous lifestyle and going the other direction is the action God requires, for one to be firmly in the middle of His will. However, getting to the place of totally surrendering to Jesus took a lot of time for me. I recently watched A minister on a television show talk about about how one can deliver him or herself from demonic attack. I love his heart for the Lord. He mentions how demons can influence and can even occupy the space of a person, even of believers. It is now clear to me that I was being influenced. One might say, well, if it is demonic attack, then how did it get in? The minister asserts that there are a few main ways that demons get inside our space, and the main ones are generational sin, trauma or fear. I certainly experienced all of these things in my life, and I believe the sin of homosexuality is in my blood because Adam and Eve sinned first, and I am their offspring. I went through tremendous periods of fear, doubt, and anxiety, and I experienced trauma at the hands of abusers who would warp the innocence of my youth. But, in the end the decision to act on my feelings is up to me.

How can one truly be born again and saved, if he or she doesn't believe the Bible, one might ask? I found that not believing the Bible and simultaneously choosing to believe that I was saved to be a contradiction, for I was selectively picking and choosing what I would believe in God's word, though He clearly says that all of His word is truth. If I remained stubborn to what God had said, I would in effect continue to be deceived by the enemy. The enemy is crafty, and he is the father of lies (John 8:44), but he is not omnipresent, omniscient or omnipotent. That is why he must send demons to do his work, for he can't be everywhere at once. After all, he is a created being. How dare he have the audacity to mislead the world into thinking he is God or anything like God. I am reminded in scripture that we are not fighting people on earth, but there is a war in our midst, a war of a spiritual nature, and men's and women's souls are the bounty. So, when I go back and look at my journey, I am clear that through all interaction with God up until that point, He was saying clearly that the issue of homosexuality not being a viable relationship dynamic in His eyes was settled. His opinion was given thousands of years ago in scripture.

It is clear to me now that same sex love is not His design. I don't believe that the fallen state of man is God's perfect will either, for it was not God's desire for Eve and Adam to eat of the tree in the Garden of Eden. I believe this state we are in will play out until the final curtain closes. God already knows the end and the beginning, for He is the alpha and omega. He knew what each of us would choose. I tell my friends all of the time that everything in life is choice. I felt as though I was designed and destined to be gay, but my love for God compelled me to seek and find out whether that belief had merit.

One might say, again, well why does my story matter? My answer would be because it is the truth that has been lived by someone in the trenches. I am not a woman who has a gay brother and is weighing in on the issue. I am someone who was pulled out of the enemy's camp with a powerful hand, so I would say my story deserves a listen. Looking back, I can say that I knew I was different from other little boys, and I somehow discerned it would be an issue later in life. I believed with every fiber of my being that God made me to be a gay man, but the Bible does not support this, and God refuted this. God has shown me that He simply wouldn't remove my desire for men. I also used to ask the question that if God is perfect and all knowing, why won't He simply remove my desire? One short answer is that God gave us free will when He made us. If He then goes and changes certain things, for example His commandments about morality, then doing so makes Him a liar. He won't go back and change what Adam and Eve did by eating the fruit. Christ's blood had to be shed, for God is holy and cannot just ignore sin. All sin required the blood payment of Christs sacrifice. He is just and holy, and we now have to do our part. I recently worked with a colleague who assumed that I was gay and asked me if I had a husband, and I responded by saying, "Yes, His name is Jesus." I then went on to explain that instead of choosing a human partner for a husband, Christ instead chose me to be part of His bride, the church. Her question opened the door for me to explain a few details of biblical marriage the way God sees it, and the question also allowed me to explain how He gave me permission to wear a gold wedding band in honor of my commitment to Him. Of course, a situation like this opens up a door for the Holy Spirit to then witness about the sin of homosexuality. God has made it clear that I must do so in a loving, patient way, just like He did with me in a process that took many years. It is now clear to me that God's intention for my life is for me to truly become my best self, the self He intended for me to become from the beginning.

This colleague was very contentious, and it was a tense conversation. I went into the bathroom to pray, saying, "Lord, sharing my story is really going to be tough, huh?" He immediately put two words in my spirit that popped into my head. He said, "REMEMBER JUDAS." I have to say that I never even think about Judas, though the other apostles may come into mind at times. I knew instantly that the Lord was giving me a very clear message. I instantly understood that just as Judas betrayed Jesus, my coworkers might turn me in to management, saying that I was proselytizing at work. God knew I was thinking I might be betrayed by a coworker. Losing my job might be part of the persecution I might have to suffer as a believer. When I exited the bathroom, I realized that He had given me the courage to continue the discussion without fear of reprisal. I knew that He was orchestrating my steps, He was in direct step with me, as evidenced by how quickly He responded to my question in the bathroom. When I exited the bathroom, I was able to stand on the word, and my colleague actually began to agree that the Bible is true.

God's answer gave me resounding comfort. I quite simply have arrived at a place where I am resolute, steadfast and unmovable in knowing that all of God's word is true, not just the parts that I don't want to believe or the parts which make my fleshly nature uncomfortable. I am so content and so elated to have more understanding of His view of sexuality in particular, and along with it, He has given me immeasurable peace.

It is becoming even clearer to me that the true state of a single person is to be in direct relationship with God Himself. I now believe that I am created, emotions and all, by the Creator, but I also believe that choices I make are key. I believe that our entire existence may come down to the notion of choice. The apostle Paul talked a great deal about sexuality, marriage and behavior in the New Testament, and he made abundantly clear that celibacy is an even higher calling than marriage. 1 Corinthians 7:32-33 talks about how a single man who cares for God is different than a married man. It says, But I want you to be without care. He who is unmarried cares for the things of the Lord - how he may please the Lord. 33 But he who is married cares about the things of the world - how he may please *his* wife.

Further, Christ said in Matthew 19:11-12 how eunuchs were highly favored by God and that some were even made that way on purpose. But He said to them, "All cannot accept this saying, but only *those* to whom it has been given: 12 "For there are eunuchs who were born thus from *their* mother's womb, and there are eunuchs who were made eunuchs by men, and there are eunuchs who have made themselves eunuchs for the kingdom of heaven's sake. He who is able to accept *it*, let him accept *it*." It is abundantly clear that this is the desired state for a single man who is not married to a woman. Paul also inferred that one should only marry if he is burning in lust. So, the ideal objective is to be separate and holy for God Himself.

I was clear now that my journey to the Southwest had come to an end, and I talked to the Lord about returning to the East coast before I put in a transfer request. My roommate had a sister whom he wanted to have move in, and I knew I wanted to be moved out of the house by the time she moved. He told me that she would be moving in the first week of October, so I asked the Lord to allow my transfer to open back to the East coast, if He was okay with my decision. Prior to my praying the prayer, the East coast had been closed to incoming transfers for well over a year! Wouldn't you know my transfer was awarded September 27th???? God is purposeful, and He will give you specific answers, if you seek Him wholeheartedly. My whole journey until now had ushered me lovingly through the continuing process of sanctification unto God Himself.

Shortly after returning to the East coast, I worked a flight abroad and went shopping with a colleague who showed me places to buy wedding rings. I had been meditating about the desire to buy a gold ring which I knew would be the symbol of a renewed heart for the Lord. I had been thinking about buying a ring for some time, and the day just before entering the gold shop, the Lord placed the story of the prodigal son in my spirit. I had been asking Him, if buying a wedding ring honored Him, so by planting Luke 15:11-32 in my heart, I now had God's answer that a wedding ring was okay. I could now tell myself as well as others that like the prodigal son, I had been joyously welcomed home. The ring for me now was symbolic of the fact that God now viewed me as having returned to Him and confirmed that I had always been part of the bride of Christ. I had found my place in the Master's arms, for I was designed to be there from the beginning.

All of the visions God gave me as well as the audible words spoken to me while awake over the course of my ten-year journey directly addressed my questions about how He views homosexuality. Curiously, all these events totaled seven in number: God said my behavior was nasty while speaking through an image of my grandmother in the first vision; God dropped me out of His hand showing His displeasure with homosexuality in the second vision; God spoke out loud to me in Europe saying that the issue of homosexuality was not okay with Him in the third interaction; God allowed the devil to deceive me when He allowed the devil to tell me that homosexuality was okay, as long as it was a monogamous union in the fourth vision; God spoke to me in the airline employee parking lot informing me that masturbation is adultery in the fifth instance; God told me to read Deuteronomy 4:2 which says never to add nor take away from His word in the sixth vision; God told me in the airplane bathroom to remember how Judas betrayed Christ in the seventh and final instance. All of these instances over time clearly showed me God's view of homosexuality. I don't completely understand the symbology of the number seven, but I know enough to recall that the Bible says that seven signifies completion and perfection. It is clear to me now that my journey seeking God's heart about the truth of homosexuality was complete.

So, I will hold firm to my decision. In essence, He wooed me, and He allowed me to fall for Him. The icing on the cake for me in my journey is that my interaction with and questions to God Himself were answered directly and also fully confirmed in scripture. I have to admit that my fleshly nature is not happy with the conclusion I have drawn from having received seven instances over the course of ten years where God allowed me a glimpse into His heart about how He feels about homosexuality. But His interaction with me is an example of how he says in scripture that we don't have the truth, because we have not asked for it. Ultimately my spirit is overjoyed, and I can say with exhaustive jubilation that I am glad He is still on the throne. My fleshly nature will simply have to fall in line with my new spirit, because it is the captain of my ship, and it gets stronger day by day.

My friends believe that I won't be happy not being in a relationship with a man, but my answer to them is that my happiness will only increase! I always thought walking away from being gay would leave a lonely void inside of me, but God has filled that space with more of Himself. I have such peace inside me now. We are created to be His and He is our portion forever. Why not start to get to know Him now before eternity starts? Why wait until the end of one's life? I say, why not start now, because there is no guarantee one will even wake to see another sunrise, especially if the person dies in their sleep like my mother did. She was right with God, so her death means having a second life in eternity with the Father. It is wonderful to have that assurance here on earth. But at least she won't have to die the second death. Christ was clear that fleeing every appearance of evil brings unbridled joy. I am choosing to rest in the peace and love of my heavenly Father, and for me that is greater than any gift a person could ever give me. It is better than gold, rubies, or money, and it is even better than being in a relationship with a human male. I believe the peace that God is giving me will fill me to a point where I will be so overflowing with love and peace that I won't even desire the love of another human being in a sexual way, ever.

People on the left might ask: How does one stop being gay, if God is displeased with homosexuality? Can one willfully choose to disobey God and avoid going to hell when he or she dies? My journey to God's truth showed me that I had to surrender completely to God and admit that I couldn't walk away from being gay by myself. No one can truly say when or how a person will come to the Lord, for justification can even happen the instant a person is taken from this existence. I believe the only way to really guarantee a spot in hell is to reject God's offer of salvation by refusing to accept His Son as personal Savior and Lord. God's love and mercy seem infinite from where I sit, and I know He will give a person myriad chances just like He did with me. One just has to be genuinely honest and seek Him. The short answer is that a person must admit first that God is right, and they are wrong. This journey of mine is one to truth, and what God has revealed to me is that the journey back to wholeness is a process. There really is no quick fix. Kylie, who gave me feedback about my dream of the old man earlier in this chapter, asked me how her nephew, who is three years old, who appeared to be gay, could be changed. I maintain that the parent must then intercede in prayer on behalf of the one who is too young to do it for themselves. Praying for the child will allow heaven to intervene by gently pushing that child onto a path where he or she will have to eventually reconcile his or her life choices against the backdrop of what kind of behavior is required to live before the presence of a holy God. Ultimately, when the child becomes old enough, he or she will face the choice and privilege to develop a fulfilling relationship with God and become born again, just like anyone else. I discovered that my real change of heart happened when I decided to let go of what control I thought I had and instead began to trust that God would take care of my brokenness over time. Ultimately, I decided to try God at His word and wait for the change that will result, as He promised.

As I mentioned earlier in the chapter, I believe gayness entered mankind through eating of the fruit in the Garden of Eden. What God has shown me through word and deed is that you combat fear and deception with truth, in essence the word of God. This is the only way. The word even says that His perfect love casts out all fear (1 John 4:18). His word is a double-edged sword that will cut the person, dividing between soul and spirit (Hebrews 4:12). I found that I had to submit to God, but I agree that submitting is not simple. I had to make the decision to die to self which is a continual process. I had to be willing to get a place where I understood and accepted that God's will was more important than my own. That is when true transformation began to take place. God changed me from the inside out, because He says faith comes by hearing, and hearing by the word of God (Romans 10:17). I continue to hear the word, read it, saturate my mind with it, and I now see gradual change happen. I was also advised by other Christians to join a church where the Bible is preached and not compromised. This decision would strengthen me to stay on the path that He would have me travel.

Real change required that I pull myself away from any influence that stood in opposition of what the Bible teaches. This meant that I had to draw a figurative line in the sand and choose to adhere to what I already knew for sure. It really required that I reinvent myself, but it was really Jesus who was reinventing me. Agreeing with Him cost me everything in which I had placed value.

At several points in my life I wanted to surrender to God, but I couldn't find the strength to do so. I sought refuge in antidepressants, counseling, sex, boyfriends, and ungodly counsel, but none of it gave me true peace. The Bible even says that sin is even pleasurable for a period of time. If a parent or guardian is looking to see change in a person who won't make steps toward God, I would say then prayer is the only thing that will allow that person to be drawn lovingly to his or her Savior for understanding. Prayer takes time, and it may even take a lifetime. Look at my example. I believed the strong women in my life prayed for me, even when I wasn't aware they were. No mother wants to give her son or daughter over to a lifestyle that God says flee from, so ultimately the prayers of the righteous women in my life definitely affected my heart in the end.

I changed slowly, and it may not have even appeared as though I was different to those outside of me, for change happened gradually. I was always taught by family that anything gained in haste will be lost the same way. So, real change will take time. How much time? Only God really knows. But, I didn't give up. God got my attention as I prayed and remained in constant meditation which allowed me to hear His voice. I am not sure through which avenue my desire for men entered, but it may have entered when I was quite a small child. I mentioned in the opening of the book that I was standing in a grocery store, desiring that the man behind us in line would be my father. It may have entered there, or it may have always been in my blood. I now know that it is not important that I discern from which avenue it came. The important work up until now for me has been in realizing that I needed to only focus on the truth to becoming whole in Jesus. Jesus name is synonymous with wholeness. Since I was seeking absolute truth, Jesus cleared my mind and allowed me to see and hear clearly. God is supreme, and He will do things in His own time. I just had to learn to trust God enough to recognize that Father would take care of everything. True love of self then blossomed, for I was willing to surrender my belief in a lie and instead begin to see myself as God did. If I can surrender and allow Him in, then anyone can. If you are reading this, you will be victorious. It doesn't matter who you are or how many mistakes you may have made. Christ is waiting for you to take one step toward Him in obedience. He will do the rest.

Scripture says that people will be influenced by this lifestyle in the last days to their detriment. Children are even being shown that it is okay to live actively as a gay person. So, homosexuality is not just a private matter between consenting adults. One huge mistake I have always made has been that of inviting and entertaining too many opinions other than God's. I now wake daily thinking about scripture, and my thoughts keep going back to my desire to seek God first, for seeking His face is its own true reward.

What I have learned is that the more I read scripture and trust God to renew my mind to believe what He says about an issue, then I continue to see a change in my behavior. Further, in reading scripture, I am becoming conformed to God's very own likeness through His Precious Son, Jesus. In Philippians 2:5, Paul says, "Let this mind be in you which was also in Christ Jesus." The old desire grew in adulthood even though I was baptized and accepted into Christ as a teenager, but real change happened inside me when I agreed with God in finally believing everything He said in scripture. It was instant. So, if the gay desire pops up now, I know it is the enemy or my fleshly nature reminding me of where I was, not where I am.

Christ was born, ministered on the earth, was crucified, buried, rose again and is now seated at God's right hand. His blood on the cross is payment for our sins. We cannot approach God except that we become covered by His blood, so if we accept Jesus as our savior, God no longer sees us as sinners but as sons and daughters. He sees the blood of His Precious Son on us, which gives us entry into His throne room. I am sure of all of these things. And, I am already noticing changes in my soul. I am overjoyed, for my spirit is now in charge, not my fallen fleshly nature. The battle is easier now, because I am leaning on Christ. I feel as though I had been in a dark room since the age of seven or so, when I first began to struggle with sexuality. I now feel as though a light has been turned on in my soul, and I can see clearly now. We are tripartite beings just like God Himself, spirit, soul and body. Everyone's spirit is dead, until it becomes alive by accepting Christ. If our spirit is not born again, then the fleshly nature is leading our lives, fulfilling our desires and leading us to make choices that are not in line with how God fashioned us in the womb.

When we accept Christ's sacrifice at Calvary, we become born again in our spirit by believing His word, the Bible, and we are forever sealed as being a child of God and will inherit heaven. It can never be taken from us. Christ's sacrifice paid all of our sin debt in full. Some Christians believe that only our past sins before becoming born again were wiped away at Calvary, but proper perspective shows that all of our sin happened after His sacrifice. Thus, the entirety of our sin was a future event, as it relates to His death which happened 2000 years ago. His blood is so powerful that it paid for all past, present, and future sin, and it is continually renewing, for it will never lose its power. So, we can never fall out of grace or favor with God in the future. All of those He has called to Himself, He will maintain. The only way a believer can lose heaven is if they reject God and deny Christ, then they will go to hell. However, once a person accepts Christ I would argue that then rejecting Him would not be an easy thing to do. If the person truly experiences His goodness, how can they reject Him? Hell wasn't created for humans; it was created for a third of the heavenly host of angels that fell and followed satan, but people will go there, if they reject God, His Son and His word.

Chapter Ten

It feels so amazing to finally have my spirit and soul and body aligned, for my body has no choice but to be obedient and follow. I do believe a person has to get to this place willingly, however. I don't believe God wants a sacrifice that is not freely given. It is also not true sacrifice, if we are harboring resentment. Also, God is a gentleman, He will not force Himself on anyone. He is clear in His word that we must seek Him, not the other way around. It certainly took me a very long time to get to this place of being willing to give up my fleshly nature for God's love. I realize that I was in denial and lacked understanding about His word. I was even uncomfortable when I would see a Bible on the airplane sitting on someone's tray table. I would flinch, for I knew it was convicting me of sin even when it was closed. I was really afraid of anything holy, because I somehow knew I was living in a way that was wrong, even though I told myself I was fine. I am now entering that peace that surpasses understanding, and the rest of my field of vision is becoming absolutely clear. The Bible suddenly makes sense to me. Ultimately, the most important thing for me in this entire journey is that I am indeed on a journey. I am seeking God, and I desire an intimate, loving relationship with Him first.

When scripture talks about delighting oneself in the Lord and He will give you the desires of your heart, I believe it is talking about this kind of revelation that I am experiencing with Him (Psalm 37:4). I believe He is referring to the new heart of flesh, not the heart of stone that had been conditioned by sin. So we begin to desire things that glorify Him, not ourselves. For example, I am noticing a desire to feed those who are hungry, as well as help the poor, homeless and orphans. I am genuinely excited about what God will do with me next. I will remain open to His voice and be obedient, for I don't know where my journey will lead next. How God chooses to do things is amazing to me, and I am amazed at how He works. I am so pleased with this new level of understanding. I have also begun to have intense visions of me healing and delivering people from oppression and bondage, with Christ acting through me. It is more than I could have ever imagined!!

I believe scripture is true, and I believe it is like an onion, with layers upon layers being peeled away, according to where we are in our level of understanding. Ultimately, walking with God is a process, a continual, daily, loving interface wherein He shows us His will, His word and His truth. I will continue to seek God for truth in everything about how He wants me to live, but His words to me are most precious, and I will treasure them as long as I live. I will no longer look to people to interpret what God is saying to me. I believe He will reveal it Himself, if I ask and He desires. Scripture is clear when it says, "ask and you will receive." God will never leave us or forsake us. That is a promise. I am finding that by doing my part and seeking His face, regardless of the personal cost, then He will reveal mysteries and pour out wisdom, so I can live and be at peace in choosing His path.

I still notice handsome men and my fleshly nature wants to engage, but I ignore it and walk the other direction now. A guy recently cruised me and gave me his phone number at Los Angeles International airport. I was talking with my coworker, and he walked up, politely interrupted and said that I had dropped a piece of paper. She asked me what it was, so I opened it, and it was his phone number, saying to call him for a date. I immediately dropped it into the trash can. I was amazed at how much strength God is giving me to navigate this new course in life. A recent colleague also said to me, "But you are still attractive, in great shape, and it's not like you weren't getting offers." I said to him that I have simply decided to change partners. This is a choice I made, and it has given my soul peace.

That persistent, still, small voice in my soul that convicted me about homosexuality is still there, but now I heed it. Now I know that I must behave differently. My focus is Christ, and I remind myself daily that it will be a war, but the battle is already won. I have so much peace in knowing this without a doubt. I believe to struggle is to live, but in so doing, it also builds character and resolve. I have to read the word which strengthens the new man inside me. As I become stronger in the spirit, the fleshly nature will be easier to conquer through prayer, fasting and meditation.

I came across a saying recently that was so poignant and said simply: If a secretary pens a letter a boss is dictating to her in his office, then whose letter is it? Some would say it is her letter. But, I believe the letter is the boss's through and through. Because the boss would then read it, approve it and sign at the bottom. Anyone reading the letter would understand that the letter houses his thoughts, feelings, and expressions, though it is written with the hand of another, who is simply an intermediary. I now choose to view the Bible the same way. For even if I don't understand all that is says, I know God is the author, and if I approach it and read it with a praying spirit, then I believe He will reveal what it means to me, even if the words on the page are not clear at first glance. I had never been taught to question scripture and somehow came to believe that we are not to question God, but I see Him quite differently now.

We are made in His image; we are intelligent, thinking, feeling, and loving creatures, and thinking beings question things. I think the questioning becomes a problem when we harden our hearts, because we don't want to accept certain answers as truth and instead think that it is okay to take liberties. I believe that God is making it clear that He will not be ignored, especially when we are clear that we are asking His opinion. I know we are created beings, like angels, and we didn't make ourselves. So, I believe it is our responsibility to go before God and ask for revelation about issues that concern our hearts. I believe I am coming to a clearer level of biblical understanding every day, and that is my goal.

If we don't seek the Lord, we may simply never enter into a better or clearer understanding of the word through our relationship without Him. For example, I think of how God told Abraham to sacrifice Isaac atop a mountain, only in the last moments to stop him and provide a ram, which was caught by its horns in the bush, as a substitute. I believe He was testing the heart of

Abraham to see what Abraham was truly made of. Of course God knows already what we will or won't do, so I believe the test is really for us to see how far we are willing to go ourselves. Do we really desire to be truly obedient? The Israelites were holy, or so they thought, but their legalism hardened their hearts in the end. They became so hard and unfeeling that they even rejected Christ, the cornerstone of our faith, who had been foretold through prophecy.

I believe God is showing me that whenever we think we have it all figured out, another layer of the onion, as it were, is peeled off. The veil in the temple was torn when Christ died, and truth is now exposed. In making an effort to consecrate my flesh, ultimately I know that I don't consecrate it, God does. What I can do in my journey is make an effort to align myself with holiness, good works, and to walk away from my flesh. Since I have arrived at a place where I simply choose not to date men, I know I am conquering my fleshly nature by being obedient to the newborn spirit inside of me. I realize that seeking a mate most of my life has caused me consternation and pain, because deep down inside, I always felt something about it must be wrong, if people said the Bible spoke against it. I simply had to find out for myself whether there was validity to the argument of people on the right.

My journey for mortal love ultimately brought me into a closer, more intimate relationship with the Creator, Himself. I believe I am simply coming to a place where I will not want earthly love, because I am more concerned with the true lover of my soul, God Himself. This sits really well with my spirit, as I now believe that celibacy is ultimately God's perfect plan for the life of a man or woman who believes that he or she was made to love a person of the same gender. After all, that is the first commandment, to love the Lord with all of one's heart, soul, and might. Yet no one really was capable of loving that way. There are many who even hate themselves, so really our belief needs to be that God is the author of love. Our loving of others should not be contingent upon how we love ourselves, but should be predicated on how God first loved us.

It seems I am getting exactly what I have been looking for all my life; I am getting a personal, loving relationship with the man of my dreams, Christ Himself. What a strange twist, that I am ending up with a husband after all, for believers are the bride of Christ, and He is the bridegroom. Writing this book has helped me in innumerable ways, and I believe that writing it enabled me to discover more about the path that God had intended for me even before time began.

I believe God directed me to write this account. My friend, Shirley even told me a year or so ago that God told her that I was writing a book, though I had never told her myself. It is clear to me now that God alone is our refuge, our peace, our first love. Christ is clear that we are to die to our fleshly nature daily. Man lives not by bread alone, but by every word that issues forth from the mouth of God (Matthew 4:4).

CHAPTER ELEVEN

❦

Walking with God is a race, but also a journey, and I know there will be twists and turns along the way. Shirley recently said to me that God revealed to her I don't need to worry about making mistakes along the way, anyway, because His will always comes to pass, regardless. Now, that sounds exactly how I know Him to sound. I remind myself that the aim of the Christian is to be like Christ. And I remind myself, how can we be salt and light in a world that is exactly like us, if the world cannot tell us apart from itself? I recently read a quote in a Christian periodical where the author said simply, "Know Christ, know change. No Christ, no change."

Christ clearly told His disciples that if we follow Him, we would have to give up something in the world. Scripture also reminds us that what we are to give up often times is that which is most precious to us. How many of us are willing to make that sacrifice? People on the left say, "Well, Christ didn't walk away from prostitutes, gamblers, and drunkards in His day." I would say that view is exactly correct. I don't believe He would shun gay people, either, but I do know beyond the shadow of a doubt He would say that we cannot do whatever we want to do with our bodies, for our bodies are the temple of the Holy Spirit. Christ was clear that He did not come to abolish the law, but to fulfill it.

If anything, He came to give us a clearer understanding, and actually expanded the laws about immorality. We have a sin nature, so we may always struggle with sin. But, I believe it is important to have a foundation for understanding what we believe to be sin and not guess. If I was an atheist and reading this book, I might be inflamed with anger at anyone who told me that being gay was not God's will for my life. However, I hope I have shown how clearly misplaced that anger is. Going a step further, God says there is no such thing as an atheist, either, for He made all of us knowing He is real (Romans 1:18-22).

I believe the gay issue will only cause more heartache for believers and unbelievers, as society becomes more accepting of homosexuality and gay marriage proliferates across the world. Gay people might believe that people who reference the Bible are making them unhappy, but God asserts that choosing a lifestyle outside of His plan for life is unhappiness by definition. God is warning us, because He loves us dearly. God is not mocked; His word is true. Sin is only good for a while, but it ends tragically. I have gay friends who say they are content, even happy and in love, but God showed me that thinking I had peace was really deception.

I believe each of us has to search his or her heart to find if we are living a life that we believe God is okay with, if we call ourselves Christians. I believe the current political and social climate wherein we are seeing countries approve homosexual and lesbian marriage has simply pushed me to examine the issue more fervently, so I can be abundantly clear about my position. I think a prudent question to ask is: Why is the gay issue becoming such a divisive issue now? Why not one thousand years ago? My answer would be that I feel that our time is getting short as a planet, and we have to choose what we believe. I believe many events are lining up in scripture, as tribulations around the world attest. My great-grandmother used to say the same thing thirty-five years ago, and some might say that I am being cryptic, reasoning like my great-grandmother. However, Christ says that people will still be given and taken in marriage when He returns.

Scripture mentions several things being in place that would usher in the return of the Messiah. The formation of Israel as a homeland, which happened in 1948, opened the door for prophecy being fulfilled in our lifetime. Scripture is clear that He will return in the manner in which He left. He ascended into heaven with His arms open wide, welcoming all to come to Him. He will descend the exact same way in bodily form, not in spirit. He will plant His feet exactly where He left, the Mount of Olives on Israel's Temple Mount. I believe that as Christians we have to always be ready, because Christ said no one will know the minute or the hour when He chooses to return. When He returns, the dead in Christ will rise first, then those of us who are still alive will never see death, but will be changed in the twinkling of an eye (1 Corinthians 15:52). We will then go to be with Him in the air, in heaven (1 Thessalonians 4:17).

My journey so far has been an interesting process of getting to this truth. I find that I have come to a certain level of understanding at times, and at other times changed my mind and reversed course.

I realize now that I have had a divided mind about sexuality my entire life, but I know He can make all things new and give me His complete peace. I know God can't abide double-mindedness (Psalm 119:113). A friend of mine recently said to me that he believed some parts of the Bible were true and others not. Interestingly enough, I always like to ask people who espouse this view, which parts do they not think are true? Interestingly enough, no one can ever tell you which parts aren't true. A metaphor I heard recently likened scripture to a stop sign. It said something like, "When approaching a stop sign, how do we determine if it is directing us to stop each time, sometimes or simply leaves it up to us as to when we want to stop?" I now view the Bible the same way. It says exactly what it means and is not subjective. Christ made it clear that if we are His sheep, then we need to heed His voice (John 10:27).

Chapter Eleven

Christ talked so much about being on solid rock. He told Peter that His church is built on solid rock and that all other ground is sinking sand. I realize now that I choose to believe as I have always believed, I simply choose to believe completely now. Just as Peter denied Christ three times when confronted on three separate occasions, we each have a chance to stand on the word or deny Him. I realize that I do not want to deny Christ, nor His message. My spirit rules over my flesh, and it wants to do God's will as He outlined in scripture. The apostle Paul talks about the dichotomy of the fleshly nature versus our spirit a lot in Romans, so I certainly understand that our continued experiences in this life will not be easy.

You may ask again: Why would I take such a journey? I would say that my respect for God was instilled in me at a young age. So, I simply had to find out for myself what God thought, given the fact I felt I was gay from birth. Gay people might say that this book simply repeats the hateful speech that Christians use to condemn gay people, but I argue it does the opposite. God's love for all creation is so amazing that He gave His only, sin-free, innocent life for ours. The first Adam gave away the keys to the earth and gave all control over to the devil. Biblical truth is not something one will understand, if he or she is led by emotions, for emotions are of our fleshly nature. God is clear that we are not to live by what we feel. We are to live by faith and by truth. Our emotions will change, the world will be shaken, but His word will never change or pass away. Adam was the ruler of this world, but when Adam sinned he gave the keys to the devil. Now, Christ is the owner once again, because His blood paid the price of the ransom on our souls. Christ, who is really the second Adam, has come and died and is alive, seated at God's right hand. The circle has been completed.

Since my heart of stone has been replaced with a heart of flesh, I know God is using me to write this expose. Even though I still notice my attraction to men, I believe God is telling me that His grace is sufficient to keep me from sinning against Him (2

Corinthians 12:9). For a time, I actually believed that if my gayness was ever taken away, I would rather die. I now realize that I am doing just that. I am learning to die to my fleshly desires. I am learning to live in Christ more and more every day. I feel a great weight lifted, as I no longer have to search to find a partner, go on dates, be rejected by potential mates, and deal with emotional games. It is beautiful to observe the change that is occurring within me. For the word says, we are to die to sin and be slaves no more, and instead become slaves to righteousness (Romans 6:18).

If I had a thousand tongues, I know I could not praise God enough for what He has already done for me in my life. So now I can live for Him, because He died for me. And the word is clear, if a parent spares the rod, he hates the child, but he who loves him disciplines him promptly (Proverbs 13:24). So, God orders our steps, even if they sometimes tend to be painful. Everything we need to live a life He is pleased with is directly in scripture. I don't believe it matters which version of the Bible a person has, for the Spirit behind the translation is the same now and forever more. There is only one source, His truth. If we are not clear about the words on the page, then we need to ask the Holy Spirit to guide us. I believe we usually have an idea what the mood or feeling of the passage is about, especially if it is about a personal issue the individual is questioning. Some stories in the Bible are allegory, some metaphor and some literal. It is not my job to unravel all the mysteries, but it is my job to be obedient to that which I do understand.

Gays might say, "Well, I don't want any part of Christ, because Christians are hypocrites; they are also in the nightclubs, bars, and bookstores just like us." My answer would be that Christ might even enter a bar, club, or bookstore, but He would be there in a much different capacity than those who are there to partake. Otherwise, how would believers meet unbelievers if they removed themselves from places that weren't holy? God meets us right where we are. Religion has misled people into believing that they have to be holy first before approaching God.

Chapter Eleven

However, because of Christ's sacrifice, we can meet God directly even though we're dirty, because Christ's blood washes us clean. It's Christ's righteousness not their own righteousness God sees when He looks at those who believe the truth.

I realize now that I have come into a time where God is showing me His word more clearly, and I am thankful for this journey. My heart is more open, raw, and more willing to follow where He leads. Regardless of where He leads, I know Christ is leading, so it will be for my good and His glory. His word is clear. For, if we are called according to His purpose, then all things will result for His glory and our good. I believe God will complete His work in me. It is clear that our bodies don't belong to us, but they are the temple of the Holy Spirit, for they were paid for with a high price, the sacrifice of God made flesh in His Son, Jesus Christ. The reality is that all human beings are called to be holy, not just some. Worshipping idols or engaging in any form of idolatry is unacceptable to God. He very clearly stated that in the next life that many will knock at the door, and He will say to some, "I never knew you; depart from Me, you who practice lawlessness! "(Matthew 7:23). I believe this will only be the punishment for a soul who committed the unpardonable sin the Bible talks about, which is rejecting Christ.

I discovered that if I willfully chose to remain in homosexuality, I was actually rejecting God, Himself, the person I said I respected and loved most in life. The Bible also says in John 6:51 that we are saved and going to heaven, if we accept Him. I posit if we are engaging in behavior that He condemns, then are we truly accepting Him? For me, it simply comes down to staring truth in the face and not blinking. Today I can make a choice to be at peace about the homosexual issue and walk away from it, for God cleared up the issue for me.

I assert that this book encompasses all of the wisdom and knowledge God has allowed me to gain thus far, as He has allowed me to question myself, others and Him directly about His views on homosexuality. It is my story, a story of my love for

God and my journey of seeking Him directly about how to live my life in a way that He is pleased with, given that I knew I was attracted to men. There has been a spiritual battle raging inside of me my entire life over sexuality, but how sweet it is to finally make a decision about what role God's own words will have in my life. I no longer have to question His law. I now believe that homosexuality displeases Him, but I believe He loves each of us so much, and I believe that each of us has the power to make a choice about how we are going to live our lives.

I will continue to ask for the courage to accept the truth about all issues, even if my flesh wants the opposite. Friends again might ask: Was the journey worth it? Did it accomplish anything? How does this help someone who is also gay and still believes that being gay is okay? I would reply that I am glad that I have not closed my heart to seeking answers, regardless of where they take me or regardless of how people respond to me. God rescued me from anxiety, depression, sexual immorality and sexually transmitted diseases, so I know that He is not going to abandon me now.

I had to face the reality of losing so-called friends, but I found that doing so was worth it, because I found my true self in the end. I realized that when my mother died, I was losing my best friend. I now realize that in losing my closest earthly friend, Christ, my Father, the lover of my soul, filled the gap and has always been there beside me, for He sticks closer than any brother. I don't think the path of life gets easier by denying gay feelings. I went down that road in my teen years and wound up becoming depressed and anxious. It doesn't work. In fact, God says that if we cast our cares on Him, He is just and able to forgive us our sins and deliver and save us. I have learned that when I am weak, then He is strong. He says His grace is sufficient, which clearly means to me that I simply need to trust Him. If someone were to ask, "Well, how does one get rid of gay feelings, if God doesn't like it?" I found that all I needed to do was to acknowledge that I couldn't do it alone. I had to be completely honest

Chapter Eleven

with God and tell Him that getting rid of my desires was too big of a job for me. He then went to work and showed me His miraculous, amazing grace which overwhelmed my heart and changed me from within. But, I know that I have to read the Bible daily and remain in prayer in order to get closer to Him in the future. Ultimately, I had to surrender completely and trust the process of becoming renewed. Walking with God is a daily thing. It is a process. It will take time.

Some might say, "Well, I talk to God, but I couldn't discern His voice." I am learning that God won't speak to me, unless He has my complete attention. I am learning that I simply have to tarry and wait on Him, until He decides to answer me. I have found that the more I spend time with Him, the more my desires change. I realize I don't want to disappoint Him, and I finally realize that my sole desire is to please God. He has shown me that He Himself will fill that void of loneliness and longing for a mortal partner, for the longing we all have is really a spiritual desire that needs to first be filled by our Maker.

I never actually would have believed it if you had told me that I would arrive here, but I am now at peace. Someone might say, "I believe your account, but what if I still want a boyfriend?" God showed me that choosing to remain in a relationship with a man put me firmly outside of His will. I now understand that Christ living in and through me makes me want to please Him.

Looking back over my journey I see that I was always concerned with wanting to be liked, but I am realizing more and more that I don't need to be concerned about what people think at all. I have found that, if I had never made the decision to ignore people, including family, then I wouldn't have cultivated the spiritual fortitude required to seek God's opinion alone. He was clear with me that His strength then rose in me, so I could stand in the face of anything. I had to ask myself that if I really wanted to discover absolute truth, could I cultivate the courage to live that truth. God says, then we will be able to share in His glory in the end, because we also shared in His pain (Romans 8:17).

I know that reading this book may scare some and anger others, but my consummate goal in writing my account was to endeavor to discover the magnanimity of God's love and His desire to usher me into the full knowledge of the truth of how vast that love is. I have learned that the only thing that scares me now is not knowing what He thinks, because knowing Creator God for myself is what really concerns my heart.

God is in charge, even though it may not look like it at times. The devil is a created being, he is on a short leash, and he is not in charge, though he wants us to believe he is. I was always led to believe the devil is fighting God to win the war of souls, but the reality is that Christ already won the battle on the cross through payment of His blood. So the war for souls rages on, but the battle is already won, if one accepts the victory. That is the point of Him shedding His blood for us for all of our sins. If we believe this fact, then we will be saved. We can then strive to run the race, make it to the end and attain the glorification of our new body which will happen instantly upon His return. The devil actually knows he already lost, so he is just trying to take as many souls to hell with him as possible, because he is the personification of pride, hatred and selfishness. Writing this book has allowed me to discover that homosexuality is a tactic in a repertoire of sin that could potentially keep me separated from a fulfilling relationship with God the Father. The devil is a real being, but I found that he truly has no power over me. If I give God a chance to love me with His transformative, healing, restorative love, I won't err in so doing. I know this message is hard to hear, but Christ said in scripture, "He who has ears to hear, let him hear!" (Matthew 11:15). It is even a harder message for me to convey, because I know more than anyone how it feels to have believed that God made me to be gay. But, even though I initially felt He made me gay, I now understand that He expects me to rise above feelings and human logic and choose His logic.

When we supplant God and make a new order, then everything will unravel. God is a God of order. He is also a God of

Chapter Eleven

increase. Homosexuality is not natural, because it does not bear fruit. God alone gets to decide this; we don't have a say. I always believed that gay people bore fruit by giving, loving, sharing, and volunteering, for example, which is true. Fundamentally, however, two men or two women can't bear children. It is God's design for a seed to bear fruit. People on the left might say, "Well, there are too many people on the planet, anyway." The argument that there are too many people living on earth for earth to sustain them may be scientifically valid. However, I am sure that all manner of cosmic, natural and unnatural signs are true indications that we are closer to the end of time than we realize.

All worldly events are lining up for Christ's return, so He says we need to keep our eyes on the heavens. So, if someone reads this book and feels that what I am saying is true, I believe God is showing them what I also was able to see. If you are asking, "How do I get born again?" I would say you just need to pray a sincere prayer, telling God you believe you have sinned against Him and you believe that He is real, you believe He sent His Son who was born, lived, died, shed blood for sin remission and was resurrected and who is now seated at the right hand of God the Father, then He heard you and has forgiven you.

If you prayed this prayer and believe it, the Holy Spirit has entered your heart, you are a believer, born again, not of water or the womb, but by the Spirit of God. You may not even feel differently. But, please remember that belief is not based on feelings. It is based on truth alone. You may not always feel the Lord's presence, but He promises He will never leave or forsake us. So, He is right inside of you and all around you, even if you don't feel Him. That is His promise! God is not man; He won't break promises. How cool is it that we have a Savior we can really trust at His word!

I am so clear now that a genuine encounter with Christ completely changed me! God wooed and wowed me continually. I have been reading my Bible daily now, and I have joined a church which shows me that I have gone to the next level in my relationship with Him. I am learning to pray without ceasing, and I believe absolutely everything He tells or shows me. I had to give up a lot, but everlasting life is the prize that taught me I know I will live again, free of guilt and pain. Eventually I will have a perfect, new body when He returns for me, and I will be free of sin and perfect, just like He is in heaven. Christ makes it clear that when we truly accept Him, there will be a transformation in us by the renewing of our hearts and minds.

I believe by being born again, we will simply start learning to see life the way God sees it. I know I am flawed, broken and imperfect, but since I am clay, I know to turn to the Potter who will perfect me. I believe God can use those who have experienced real hardship the best. You may say, "Well, okay, maybe I agree with your assertion, but I want to have children. How do I do that, if I am a guy and can't marry a guy?" I feel God would be pleased with me deciding to adopt a child, since I am not married. There are so many children in need of a loving home, so love is really the required ingredient. I even recall how Christ was once at a house and was told that His mother and brothers were outside, and His response was "For whoever does the will of My Father in heaven is my brother and sister and mother" (Matthew 12:50). He made it abundantly clear that our real family are those who believe God's word. After all, children all belong to God anyway. How many times do you see children turn out in ways their parents abhor or can't understand? The truth is, we are God's children. Adults are only the baby sitters. Children have a soul He gave them at birth. It did not come from the birthing parents.

You may ask, "Will my journey from here on in be easy?" I would say no, I don't believe it will, because some other issue will arise, for which we will need an answer. Plus, scripture is clear that when we align ourselves with the will of God, hell gets nervous, ramps up action and orchestrates attacks against us. But, God is with us, so we have nothing to fear. So many of us think that we will have a few more days or years to live before we have to walk away from certain behaviors, but tomorrow is

Chapter Eleven

not promised for any of us. Even the next five minutes are not promised.

I simply ask God to give me the courage to face whatever He needs me to face during the course of my life. He already warned us that we cannot do these things alone. My journey is in the palm of His hand. I am indebted to Him in a way that I can never repay, but I can certainly start by honoring Him in believing all that He says. Thankfully, His love is a gift. By taking this journey, it feels good to finally know what it feels like and sounds like to hear God's voice directly in my spirit as well as out loud, instead of just having an inkling of what He might be saying. I now firmly believe that God wants each of His children to seek Him, to desire a relationship with Him first, and to treat others with love and respect.

After all, when I think about it, this is exactly what Christ told people who asked Him which commandments were to be obeyed, since we are no longer bound by the Old Testament. His reply was to love God with all of one's heart, soul, and mind, and to love one's neighbor as oneself.

Some may ask again, "How does this book help someone make peace with being gay?" I would say that my experience may only spark more questions for a gay person who says they don't believe in Jesus or God. I believe that if someone is gay and loves the Lord, my experience of examining scripture and talking to God deserves at least a cursory glance from anyone who seeks to live correctly before Him. I found that believing I had peace while living an active gay lifestyle to be an illusion, for deep down inside, there was nothing but uncertainty about God's views on homosexuality. Confession and repentance are really what are required for true peace. My friend Cathleen once told me that she believed God was using me much like the messengers of old. She used the analogy of a person standing at the gate, the entrance to a city or town, who warns passersby that this city must be avoided. I do agree that God allowed me to write this book, so I could find out for myself that scripture is true and inerrant.

God cares so much about us that He always sends people to confirm the truth, so we can use that information to make correct choices. He feeds the birds and clothes the flowers of the fields, and shields them from the rain. How much more does He love us? I have found that I don't believe each of us is created to be married with children. Some of us are created to be direct spouses of God Himself. I actually believe this to be a higher calling than being married to a flesh and blood partner. If we love God, then I believe we would want to find out what it means to be obedient to His will for our lives. It has now become abundantly clear to me that God first contacting and speaking to me in the form of my deceased grandmother was the crucial juncture in Him convicting my heart that the Bible means what it says. The Bible is clear how the world is supposed to work, that God alone is creator, and how things are ordered. We know that male goes with female, eggs are hatched, and that the seasons change, for that is His design. In light of people being allowed to marry the same sex, which the Supreme Court recently made legal, God reminded me that He was abundantly clear when He spoke to me regarding His view on homosexuality.

God's design is for each of us to have a fulfilled, loving, committed relationship with Him first. Understanding and being closer to God is not something I would ever want to miss out on by remaining in a behavior He says to avoid. Sin demands a sacrifice, and animal sacrifices of times past were only a shadow of the real sacrifice, Christ's death at Calvary, so that we could all have a direct relationship with Him. I wouldn't trade that for the world. He alone is my inheritance. I now have my answer. Upon dying, I want God to say to me, "Well done, My good and faithful servant," when I finally leave earth to be with Him.

CONCLUSION

In closing, I can say that I have imparted every tidbit of information that the Lord has shown or told me as it relates to His view of homosexuality. I found that living a homosexual lifestyle is not God's will or purpose. I found that truly allowing my heart to be open before Him required that I have a willingness to suspend all worldly knowledge and exhaustively strive to see His point of view. In doing this I was able to walk away from being gay on His strength alone knowing that I had finally found the truth about how a single man is supposed to live before God and man. It was at this juncture in my understanding that I truly began to die to self, and I began to live the life of the risen Christ inside of me.

Upon finally reading the Bible to completion for the first time in 2004, God convicted my heart of sin in general and of homosexuality in particular. He let me know lovingly, patiently and tenderly that loving a man is not His will. Because I was at a place spiritually where I was seeking Him and asking for an answer about how to live correctly before Him, He allowed me to enter into a more intimate relationship with Him. If you're still saying, "Well, I don't believe He is real, what do I do?" I have found that the most important thing I have ever done in my life thus far was to seek the truth in knowing for myself that He loves me individually. I found that being saved and accepting Him as

Lord of my life is what really set me on course to get answers to the other questions my heart was asking Him.

I now accept that as a believer I will not understand all that God does while I am alive, and I may not understand His view about many issues until I meet Him face to face. Yet in concluding this book, I can say that I will simply do the best I can to listen and be obedient to His voice in my heart while I am alive. Even if I fail in my attempt to reach the heights He created for me, heights He imagined even before the world was formed, I will serve Him the remainder of my days. I will consciously continue developing a more intimate, loving relationship with the one and only wise true God: my Father, my Husband, my King, my Protector, my Deliverer, my Refuge, my Strong Tower, my Way Maker, my Inheritance, my Provider, the Maker of the universe, God Almighty.

I pray my journey encourages your heart,
Stuart

CPSIA information can be obtained
at www.ICGtesting.com
Printed in the USA
BVHW07s0135260718
522550BV00002B/16/P